ASSUMPTIONS OF A POOR MAN'S PRINCESS

A novel by

Arnetta Quarles

PublishAmerica
Baltimore

First printing

Softcover 9781462621460
PUBLISHED BY PUBLISHAMERICA, LLLP
www.publishamerica.com
Baltimore

Printed in the United States of America

Dedication

To

Edwin (Uncle Tiny) (Shorty) Chambers, Sr.
Sunrise 1940 - Sunset 1986

Evelyn (Cousin Evelyn) Jones
Sunrise 1912 – Sunset 2006

Melissa Anne Taylor
Sunrise 1962 – Sunset 2010

in who's eyes I could do anything.

Suzanne –
Your testimony will
forever encourage me!
[illegible]

ASSUMPTIONS OF A POOR MAN'S PRINCESS

Chapter One
KENDAL GROVE

On the afternoon of the first Sunday in June of 1935, best friends Isaac Howard and James Carter stood side-by-side watching those who made their hearts sing. Isaac turned to his friend placed his right hand upon his left shoulder, and said, "Look at your little man and my little lady, and look at the two most beautiful women in the world, to whom we happened to be married. Are we not the two luckiest men in the world?" Knowing what was said was not in the form of a question but a factual statement. James not taking his eyes from the picturesque scene replied, "There can be no other men as blessed as we."

In the churchyard, Lethea Howard and Bertha Carter watched their children scramble about them as they awaited indication from their husbands as to what the remainder of the day would hold for them. At the invitation of Reverend Joe, James' father, a guest preacher was scheduled to give the message for the afternoon service. This allowed James, Bertha and their son Charles, nicknamed Chaz by his grandfather, too spend a few hours away from the church with the Howard's. As Lethea looked about the crowd, she spotted her husband and the pastor above them on the incline. She was familiar with the expression on their faces, and said to her best friend Bertha, "Oh no, look forward to a great big old bear hug anytime soon. They have got that luckiest man in the world look again." "I think they have it backwards, we are the lucky ones, or should I say blessed ones," said Bertha. Calling to the children, Lethea reached into her purse and withdrew a flowery embroidered handkerchief filled with several pieces of hard candy. "Take your pick," she said as the children's glowing faces loomed over the handkerchief. "I think I will take the green one," Lenora said to her mother. "You always take the green ones like I always take the orange," said Chaz. "Your turn Ricky, you can have five pieces today," Lethea said to the little boy who was never far from Chaz. After Ricky made his choices, she folded the handkerchief and placed it back into her purse. Then came a familiar cry she heard from her daughter, "Give it back Patricia!" Lethea turned around in time to see Patricia pop the green candy into her mouth. "It's all right Lenora there is more from where that came." She retrieved the handkerchief from her purse and opened it for her daughter to select another piece of candy. Then offered what was left of the candy to Patricia. As usual Patricia only took the green pieces that were left. Whatever Lenora wanted or had, she wanted it all the more. Lethea folded her handkerchief again, put it back into her purse, and walked over to Bertha and a group of ladies in the churchyard. Lenora skipped off in the opposite direction to rejoin Chaz and Ricky in play. Patricia moved far enough away to watch all of the goings-on of those in the churchyard, and to enjoy the taste of her green treasures alone.

All of the women are clucking like chickens, she thought, especially the Chadwell sisters. Victoria Chadwell Watts is still telling everyone that big lie. She's telling people that Mr. Bailey went to New York to find better work and when he gets settled he'll send for them. Why would he leave to find better work when he had a good job as the Assistant Director of Winton's Funeral Home? Other than Reverend James and his wife Bertha, Patricia was the only one who knew the truth about Bailey leaving Kendal Grove. Bailey had come to the clear-cut decision that he wanted to live, and in order to live he had to run away to save his life. His wife of fifteen years and her phony sister had driven him to beyond his breaking point. "I can't take it here anymore, Victoria," said Bailey. "I've had it up to here," describing his point by placing his right hand under his chin and grabbing his neck, "and you are choking me to death." "What are you talking about?!" Victoria demanded. "Stop packing! What are you doing?! You can't leave me! "Stop packing! Where are you going?! What am I to do?!" "Hell, if I care. You told me that you didn't need me, so why don't you live off what your Sweet Daddy left you? The man has been dead since 1927. It is 1936, Victoria! Why don't you get rid his clothes? You still have his musty clothes hanging in his closet along with the rest of his junk. You have his room set up like a shine, he wasn't no saint!" She stepped back dumbfounded. "Bailey you stop talking down Sweet Daddy that way, and you used a cuss word in my house!" "Yes, I did Victoria and it's a miracle that I'm not a drunkard living as long as I did in your house! I know a few more cuss words, do you want to hear them?" "No, no Bailey! What about our son Hector?" "Believe me, leaving my son is my only regret, but if I stay with you it will kill me. You and your sanctimonious sister make me sick!" "What did I ever do to you and why are you belittling my dear, sweet sister in that way?" "You two are evil! If you look the word "evil" up in a dictionary your pictures would be slapped right up next to the word." "It's Mabel you're leaving me for! You are leaving me for that common wench who goes to bed with every married man in Kendal Grove and grins in your face!" "Mabel? I've had nothing to do with her. No, it's you always talking about and criticizing other people. Constantly pulling everything and everyone down to the point where nothing and no one is good enough for you. I don't believe there is a good thought in you about anyone. You treat our son like he's a girl and you won't allow me to spend any time with him. Other men have time with their sons and do things like play ball, hunt and fish. But not me, he's got to be up under you and that phony, piano teaching, moose of a sister of yours. "And let me tell you girl." Isn't that what you say? "Well girl, I think you'll need to have a seat for this one." You know the times, twice to be exact that your dear sweet sister, Leslie, was having those heavy menstrual flows and we had to rush her to Doctor Mitchell's office? They wasn't no heavy menstrual flows, they was miscarriages. I know what I am talking about. How many years did I work at the hospital before I started working for old man Winston's funeral home? Not only was she having miscarriages but she making herself do it. She done been to that root lady more than once." "Root Lady? That's nonsense! We don't believe in no hoodoo-voodoo." "How do you know Victoria? You don't know everything. Think about it Victoria, when did your sister ever cook up a recipe in your kitchen and wouldn't let you taste it? You tried to taste it and she refused you, and ate it all herself with the excuse that it wasn't good enough yet. Both times the next morning, what happened, heavy menstrual flows?" Victoria, taken aback by his perception could do nothing. "Yea, you've finally got it, your sister is a sneak and she had you fooled! Now ring the bell, ding, the train has pulled into the station! Close your mouth darling." Bailey touching the bottom of her chin to close her mouth broke her trance. "Stop it Bailey, you are a liar!" "Am I? I can't rightly say who the father or fathers are, but your sister tips out at night while you're asleep." "No she doesn't, no she doesn't!" She repeated hysterically while banging on his chest with both fists. Bailey had never seen his wife in such a thither – her hair was in a free falling mess. Normally her long and straight auburn hair was neatly combed and carefully rolled into a bun that sat at the nape of her neck. Her voice was consistently controlled even when she was dispelling her venomous gossip. This was something new and he liked it. He felt a tightening in his groin and his heart beating faster, but decided to abandon the notion to take hold of her. For this time with Victoria, the very first time, he was in control. "Good-bye my darling, hug and kiss my son for me. Make sure you tell your nasty sister I didn't have any words for her." Victoria was left lying on her bedroom floor with tear soaked dress sleeves. Her nose was pink and still running and her eyes were burning, puffy and almost swollen shut. Her head and heart were rapidly pounding and she felt as if they could burst. She laid there and cried for what seemed like hours. What was she to do? Then it came to her, all there was to do at that moment was to dry her tears, blow her nose, and get up, walk into the living room, and close the front door left open when her husband departed. As she closed the door the tears returned.

It was the banging on the front doors that caught Patricia's attention sitting on the Carter's back porch steps, waiting for Chaz.

She recognized the distraught voice frantically disclosing its account. Not that she was interested in the dull lives of those in Kendal Grove, or in this particular incidence, Victoria Chadwell Watts, however, the distress in her voice intrigued Patricia. She entered the back door and inched closer to the swinging kitchen door that lead to the dining room as to better make out what was being said. "He left me, she screeched. Bailey's gone! What am I to do? Bertha, you and James must help me. I'm begging you." What? Patricia thought. Before Patricia knew it she had sprung through the kitchen door into the dining room. "Please excuse us Patricia, we have much to discuss with Mrs. Watts," said Bertha. "There, there sister, now get up from your hands and knees. Come on now stand up, we'll take it to the Lord together," said James as he and Bertha assisted Victoria to his study. Patricia was out of the dining room as fast as she entered it. She could hardly control the glee of seeing the high and mighty Victoria Watts brought to her knees. The witch, she thought, the old nasty, ugly witch is finally getting hers. And I got some more to tell her one day. Patricia danced all the way back to the porch steps to sit and wait for Chaz.

Although she hated the Chadwell sisters, Patricia hated Lenora all the more. She wished Lenora would drop dead or disappear then she could take her place. To Patricia, Lenora had everything. She had the prettiest and nicest mother, the most handsome father, and the prettiest dresses. She even had Charles (Chaz) Jones Carter, the cutest boy and his best buddy in the whole wide world, Ricky Stone, to play with at will. If that wasn't enough, Chaz had to go around telling everyone that he was going to someday marry Lenora, because she was the prettiest and nicest girl in the community. It seemed that everyone wanted it that way because they were paired together in the annual Tom Thumb weddings at church. While she was treated as second best and chosen to walk down the isle with Ricky Stone. Patricia liked Ricky, but she hated the fact that she was paired with another child from the Hill. She hated Tom Thumb weddings, as she did every event which involved the church and raising money for it. How stupid was it to make little children dress up and imitate grownups as bride and grooms with bridesmaids, best men and all to raise money? She hated the fundraisers about as much as she hated church; all of it the bake sales, fish fries and the endless chicken dinners. The interest she had in attending church or for that matter school was to look at the preacher's son, and the cutest acolyte Chaz Carter. At the age of nine, Patricia knew exactly what she wanted, and her mind was made up to have it. She knew within her heart that the person Chaz would marry someday was her, because the only way that Lenora Howard was going to marry Chaz Carter was over her dead body. She chewed and downed the last bit of candy, rubbed her hands together to rid them of the tiny green specks, and walked up the hill towards home where her grandmother was waiting. She knew her grandmother had witnessed the candy incident and she knew what was coming after that. On her way up the hill Patricia thought, why did they have to live on the Hill? Her grandmother, Minnie Haynes, was once a teacher and a resident. And for most of her life she had been somebody in Kendal Grove. How Patricia hated Lenora and how she hated living on the Hill.

In a rural community with a population of seven hundred and thirty-five located within Chrystol County, Maryland sat Kendal Grove. The various fruit tress overflowed at harvest time and the forests abounded with deer, rabbits, squirrels and wild turkeys, and for those who weren't as particular and wanted meat on the table there were possums, raccoons and turtles. The fishermen could count on nearby waterways chocked full of trout, bluegill sunfish, yellow perch and both smallmouth and largemouth bass. Blessed with abundance the ominous blight of the depression slightly scuffed the community. Originally established to provide housing for freed slaves off the land of the former plantation owners, it's nestled in the middle of where the property lines of four farms end. Kendal Grove sits adjacent to the City of Franklin, a predominately white township founded by one of the of the largest plantation owners in Chrystol County. Its population of fourteen hundred has a courthouse, police chief and two officers, two banks, Franklin Commerce and Franklin Farmers and

Merchants, two clothing stores, hardware and feed store, a diner and two restaurants. The restaurant with the Italian, pronounced I-Talion, theme features as its special spaghetti with meat sauce. The special prepared by locals who have never traveled outside the city limits of Franklin serve boiled boxed spaghetti noodles covered in warmed canned tomato sauce with a slice of Italian bread on the side, which at times is substituted with French bread and herald as a delightful feast.

The African Methodist Episcopal Church of the Heavenly Father is the focal point of Kendal Grove and is the host to the annual Camp Meetings. Where people come from miles around, during the last month of the summer, to worship and praise the Lord. It also boasts a practicing physician, general store, barber shop, funeral home and restaurant. There is also a lodge and social clubs for both men and woman. Within the community there are three neighborhoods housing three different classes of people who seldom or never make acquaintance with one another. The Residents are the affluent land and home owners who make the decisions concerning the community as a whole. The Hill People are those less fortunate and the have nots, and the Pickers of Picker's Woods are the have nots of the have not. A definite distinction between the ladies and the women of Kendal Grove is evident as the ladies of Kendal Grove are held in high esteem. Many had no more than an eighth grade education but know how many pounds are in a tonnage, how many dozen are in a bushel, how many canning jars are needed for a bushel of butter beans, how many cups, teaspoons or tablespoons are needed for their delectable culinary concoctions. The majority of the concoctions are committed to memory but when a recipe is requested and passed on to another the precise ingredients are calculated and the measurements are written out to precision. Good penmanship is a must and they take pride in the knowledge of knowing their mathematical figures, their personal appearance and the keeping of their immaculate homes. They also take pride in their family's wellbeing, the community and everything they touch. Brand new hairdos, suits or dresses, hats, gloves with matching purses and shoes are a must. Depending on the season fine hand woven shawls, fox or mink stoles, or lamb cashmere coats are worn. Lipstick, eyebrow pencil and face powder are applied to their faces and their bodies are perfumed and patted down with scented talcum powder. (With extra talcum powder added under the breast, around the waist and buttocks to avoid chaffing, of the skin when the long lined girdles are tightly zipped to compliment an hour glass figure.) For some, the closest they can get to an hour glass figure is in their imaginations. Nevertheless, on Sunday morning all is in place to sashay into the church, sit in their designated pews with their family and listen to the word of God. When a lady of Kendal Grove passes by men, young or old, deep within erroneous conversation they'd stop. Those sitting stand, and all hats are removed, until she is out of earshot before their conversation is resumed. There are some things that men discuss which should never be mentioned in the presence of a lady. Mrs. Minnie Haynes was one of those ladies.

"I saw you take that candy," Minnie said as her granddaughter stood sheepishly on the opposite side of the screen door. "You ought to have been glad, I would have had to go over twenty or thirty people in the churchyard before I got to you." "Shoot Granny she could have gotten some more candy," Patricia shot back entering the house. "You could have asked for some instead of being rude and greedy. Lethea would have been more than happy to have given you more candy. You don't have to take, Pattycake. Girl, let people offer things to you. Must I keep telling you that? Stop taking other people's belongings, it's not right, and I didn't raise you that way. Keep it up and I will start letting my strap do the talking. Why are you so nasty to Lenora anyhow? She is such a nice and polite." "I hate her!" Patricia abruptly shouted, cutting off her grandmother in mid sentence. "How can you have so much hate for someone who hasn't done anything to you?" "Because I hate her that's why, I just do." "Oh, Pattycake you're too young to know about hate. Hate is ugly and vile and can eat you up inside. It can cause you to hurt others for no reason but most of all, hate can cause you so much grief and pain you eventually hurt yourself worst of all in the long-run. Hate can take your life from you little girl." "I know why I hate her," Patricia replied growling and startling her grandmother. "How come she must have everything when I am prettier and lighter than she is?" Minnie shouted, "What!" "I am light and she is so bla." Before Patricia could complete her explanation she felt the full strength of the blow from the back of her grandmother's hand against her mouth. Never before had she been hit with such force. The outside and the inside of her lips stung and her teeth began to throb. Because she said the obvious, she was in pain. She was lighter skinned than Lenora and had longer and thicker hair. Why was she at the brunt of her grandmother's fury? "What did I do, what did I say Granny?" Patricia asked. "You opened your mouth like a low life good-for-nothing trash child. Don't you ever let me hear you call nobody darker than you black! If they were born dark then that is what the Lord intended, so that makes it fine. It doesn't make a bit of difference if a person is darker than you. They are Negro and we are Negro too, and that makes us all the same, light, dark or in between. Your grandfather was black as tar and at that time there was none around as good looking as he was. He was a God fearing, strong, proud and loving man who had it all and he had me. Your daddy was a very light skinned man, same as me. He was one of the worse men that I have met until this day. A person's skin color doesn't make a difference. The difference is what a person has in their heart. Pattycake girl, you had better fix your heart. I don't know where you are getting this mess from, or who or what you think you are. You must think you're a princess. Well, let me tell you something, the only kind of princess you'll be with those nasty ways is a poor man's princess. You are too little to be so nasty." Patricia knew not to respond. What could she say, if anything, to get her point across to her grandmother who too adored that little black wench, Lenora. She left the kitchen and entered the small room next to the kitchen which served as her bedroom. Her mouth was still tingling from her grandmother's blow and she wondered what her life would have been like if her mother had married someone else instead of her father. Maybe her mother might still be alive, her father too. Dick Wynn, her father was good looking. She knew that from the picture of her parents Granny kept in the front room. In addition, she had overheard many times ladies at the baseball games and in the speakeasy parking lot talk about her daddy's good looks, as well as some other things she couldn't fully understand. She also overheard them speak of her mother, Patsy, in hushed tones. Shake their heads from side-to-side while looking in her direction, as if they pitied her and her grandmother. But Patricia didn't care, she knew that her father had forced her mother into the car with him on the night they were killed, and that he had been drinking heavily. She also knew that her granny still hurt inside, because she never got to say good-bye to her baby, her only child. Patsy's casket could not be opened at the funeral. Patricia didn't care what the ladies said, or for that matter, what anyone said. She knew all of the stories about her parents and their arguments and how unkind her daddy was. What she didn't understand was, if he was so mean, why did so many ladies like him? On more than one occasion she overheard her uncle Paul, her father's drunkard brother say, "Did you ever see so many women cry at a man's funeral and none of them was kin? He must have been a L-O-V-E-D man." He placed emphasis on the word "loved" and then he and whomever he was speaking to burst into laughter. When they noticed she was present they would straighten-up and act serious about one thing or the other. She didn't care about her Uncle Paul, the only other living relative, or what he said either. It was as if she had never known her parents anyway. Only two years old when they died, Granny was the only parent she had known.

At the age of nine, Patricia liked to observe some of the ladies who came out to the baseball games. She took note of those who frequented the speakeasy for guidance on how to be a grown-up. They seemed to have more fun drinking liquor, chatting, laughing, dancing, kissing and hugging on men and sometimes fighting the same men. On the other hand, the women at church or those who attended the Woman Society meeting's her grandmother dragged her to monthly, were stuffy and boring, and seemed to have sticks stuck up their backs. She was convinced that the men and women who lived on the Hill and hung around the speakeasy had the most fun. That is probably why her mother married a Hill man, because he was more fun than the other men she socialized with. She hated living on the Hill, because she knew the residents looked on them as dirt. The only reason her grandmother was accepted by the residents was because she wasn't raised on the Hill and neither was her grandfather. Minnie in her early years a teacher, moved to the Hill after the loss of her husband and suffering a severe illness. With the cost of doctor bills, Granny could no longer continue making the mortgage payment of $65 a month on the lovely house where her mother was born and raised. Dick and Patsy also lived with Granny, but Dick refused to work and Patsy scarcely made enough money running errands for the residents to feed the four of them. A short time after they received the court order that the bank was taking the house, Patricia's parents died in the car accident. The talk of the residents was that the reason Minnie Haynes was still alive was because she had to get out of her sickbed to care for her grandbaby, Patricia. Shortly after the loss of Patricia's parents, they found a small house on the Hill big enough for the two of them. Out of respect for Minnie and for her contributions to the community, the twenty-two members of the Men's Temple Lodge, headed by Isaac and James, refurbished the little Hill house to resemble the home she left behind. A modern kitchen, indoor plumbing, a bathroom, a window seat, chair railings, ceiling and floor moldings, and Moorish door frames were added inside. The outside of the house was freshly painted white and a two seated swing was added to the front porch. A walkway, shrubbery and a white picket fence was added to complete the homey look and feel. Minnie took in laundry and ironed for the residents of Kendal Grove and for the neighboring white township of Franklin to support them financially. Patricia also hates that her grandmother has to wash and iron other people's dirty rags to feed and clothe them. Why wasn't Isaac Howard her father? If he was he would be a living father and Granny would no longer have to work, she reasoned. Why did Lenora have to have the good and living daddy? "Even the dirty little Ricky gets to spend more time with them than I do," she said to herself.

Ricky loved the Howard's and the Carter's, they treated him good and he always felt welcomed. They didn't treat him like he was from the Hill. Other Hill children were not allowed to enter the general store or any other place among the residents without a chaperone. Ricky Stone on the other hand was trusted and he was unrestricted in his movements. He once overheard a church lady say, "Those Hill children, you don't ever know what they will do. I don't let any of my children sit next to them or talk to any of them that might come to school. They're dirty, stupid, steal, lie and they're loud and rude. Those children are heathens and have no home training." Another lady said, "They are wild, like some wild animals that have been turned loose." All the ladies nodded in agreement. Ricky was allowed to sit with his best pal Chaz at church, play with him and eat and sleep over at his house. He was also allowed to play with Lenora at her house or at her father's general store. Ricky was definitely treated differently than the other children who lived on the Hill. He was aware of it and the other children on the Hill were aware of it too. Chaz's grandfather the Right Reverend Joseph Charles Carter, affectionately known as Reverend Joe, would playfully say, "Ricky Stone, solid as a rock. Don't let anybody turn you to the left or turn you to the right, keep your feet firm boy. Plant them feet, stay solid Stone, solid as a rock." Old Reverend Joe was the first man Ricky could remember displaying kindness toward him. Ricky did not know his grandfather, but he knew he had been Reverend Joe's best friends since they were boys like he and Chaz. His father, Macabee, called Mac by his scalawag buddies and everyone else who lived on the Hill, was renowned throughout Chrystol County for his foul mouth and furious fists. Apparently, he sought the same qualities in his woman. Young Ricky was accustomed to being awakened in his bed by loud arguments and sounds of breaking glass or furniture at any time during the night. Although, his father possessed no signs of reverence, he was afforded a great deal of respect. Or at least that is what his father thought. Ricky discerned at an early age that people cowed to his father out of fear not respect. That is except for Reverend's Joe and James and Mr. Howard. It was the opposite for them. The only indication Ricky could see that his father had any decency was when he was in the presence of his best friend's fathers and Reverend Joe. It was due to Macabee's ill temper and lack of regard for himself and others that drove his mother away. From what Ricky could gather about his mother leaving, she had a choice to stay and be beaten to death or leave and have a chance at life. She chose the later and left her four year old son with his father. He remembered his mother and had not seen her pretty face in five years. How pretty she was though most of the time her face was bruised and swollen from his father's fists. He had no ill feelings toward her about leaving him behind, if she had taken him, Macabee would have hunted them down like dogs and most likely would have killed them both. Unlike his father's present choice of women, the only reason his mother fought was to protect him, in no way did she ever provoke an argument or fight. Macabee drank heavily and fought others at will, yet he never touched Ricky and neither did his female friends. One could say he practically ignored the child, except that he slept in a clean bed at night and what little clothes he had were kept clean and neatly pressed.

Chapter Two
THE STORE

Lenora, Chaz and Ricky were staring into the pickle barrel trying to decide which pickle to choose when Patricia walked into Howard's General Store. "Where is your Daddy, pickle nose?" Patricia asked Lenora. "Lenora doesn't have a pickle nose, her nose is perfect," said Chaz, "and Uncle Isaac is in the back." "He is not your uncle," said Patricia. "I know that but he and my father are like brothers." "Like brothers? Then you can't marry Lenora, because she's your kin." "Oh, yes I can silly, because she is not my real kin." Patricia rolling her eyes at Lenora turned away. "I am going to get him, I am going to have Chaz Carter, he is mine," she said under her breath marching to the back of the store in search of Lenora's father. "What can I help you with Miss. Patricia?" Isaac asked. "My grandmother, wants to know if her special order has come in yet?" "No, little Miss. Tell your grandmother I do suspect it to come in tomorrow or the day after. And for you asking so nicely for her, here is a peppermint stick just for you." "Oh, thank you, Mr. Isaac. That's the flavor I like best." Patricia smiled so hard her cheeks pulsated. How she wished he were her daddy with his handsome face, white teeth, broad shoulders, wavy hair and smooth dark skin. For a moment she pretended he was only to turn around and see Lenora standing in front of her smiling. Her special moment was over for sure as he brushed past her and reached out to embrace his daughter. Patricia could not leave the store quick enough. Lenora spoiled her joy at every turn. One day, she thought, I will have everything I want. She will have Chaz, and Lenora won't.

In the store one could hear the footsteps of each customer on the wooden floor as they went about searching for items to place in their kersey sacks to purchase. The store sold fresh meat, poultry and produce from local farmers at retail. The jellies, jams, pies, fruit cobblers and canned fruits in jars were supplied by Miss. Dottie. Grain for human consumption and grain for livestock was also sold. Mops, brooms, pails, household hardware and hardware for animals, face creams, shaving powder, medicines for pain and baby colic, and hair tonics were sold too. Not much in the line of clothing was offered other than overalls, dungarees, gingham dresses and cheaply made cotton day dresses. However, catalogs by the dozens were available to order such. The latest 78 records that made the Hit Parade and recordings of songs that did not were sold, and a telephone was installed for community use at a small fee. What he didn't sell was the byproduct of Ludlum, Doctor Feel Better Medicine. His only other competition was the Whatnot Salesman, Mr. Johnson, who sold his wares from his horse drawn cart. Mr. Johnson, a stubby and unshaven man, with horse and wagon made his living traveling the dirt roads of Kendal Grove and nearby Franklin peddling his goods. He peddled pots, pans, books, pulp magazines, chewing gum, scarves, neck ties, five cent earrings, bracelets and rings and $1 watches; toilet water and aftershave lotions. His best selling item before it was banned, Doctor Goods Feel Better Medicine. Other than that the nearest general store was in the City of Franklin where they didn't take much to serving Negro customers.

Lenora often thought of her grandfather Sam and how he would talk about spitting right on the dirt floor of the store before her father bought it. "Can you believe little girl that this floor was a dirt floor?" Sam said pointing to the floor. "When your father bought it, some people acted like he was committing a crime by putting in a wooden floor. The folks around here didn't see a need for no wooden floor in a store. See all the old men used to come in here to sit around this here old stove. It didn't have any bricks around it then, and it wasn't all shinny like it is now. There used to be this old nasty dingy pot that used to sit right here next to it, called a "spittoon". You see a lot of men like to chew tobacco, see that is something you wouldn't know about, because a lot of women folk around here see it as a bad habit and don't like their men to chew that stuff. Well, anyway, sometime in the winter when the men would spit. See they had to spit the juice out because they couldn't swallow it. Don't make that face. I told you women folk think it's bad, and you are a little woman folk. Let me tell you, when it was cold outside the men would be chewing and have to spit, come time they would miss that thing, called a spittoon, and hit the stove. Hot Dog! That stuff would sizzle, like when you put something wet into hot grease in a frying pan? You could hear it go sssssssss. See when your daddy got this store, your grandmothers and your momma wouldn't hear of having no men spitting all over the place. So what they did was they convinced him to put in a wooden floor and to put bricks around the stove." "Which way do you like it best granddaddy?" "I like it both ways. I guess? Sometime I kind of miss the old men spitting on the floor. There were a lot of good old stories told right here on this spot. Then other times I like it the way it is because it belongs to my son. You know what?" "No granddaddy. What?" "The pickle barrel is still in the same place, and the men old and young alike still come listen to the baseball games broadcasted on the radio. So, I guess it's alright the way it is, after all."

Chapter Three
SASSY'S PLACE

Sunday afternoon during the summer months in Kendal Grove were never dull. There was something to do for everyone, picnic lunches, afternoon church services, family gatherings and pick-up baseball games. For those who were not interested in family oriented fun there was Sassy's Place. Her specialty was bar-b-que pork chops with fried apples, mashed potatoes, collard greens with pickled water melon rinds on the side, and a slice of pecan pie topped with homemade vanilla ice cream for dessert. Despite prohibition beer and moonshine, distilled at a nearby undisclosed supplier, was served in canning jars. "Critters" was the password you had to utter in a sentence in order for it to be served. Alternatively, coffee, tea or water came with the meal. Sassy's was open seven days a week, 11:00AM until 2:00AM, except on Sunday when it didn't open until 3:00PM out of respect for the preachers, Reverends Joe and James and their church. Otherwise her place was jumping with live entertainment and filled to capacity with customers. Though Sassy's place was three-fourths of a mile down the road from the church it was believed that if you stood in the middle of the road on any given Sunday evening, at an even distance between the church and Sassy's, in one ear you would hear people jumping, hollering and screaming, praising the Lord at an evening church service. In the other ear you would hear people jumping, hollering, screaming and fighting, praising the devil at Sassy's Place. Once on the walk home from church on the other side of the road, naturally, as Patricia and her grandmother were passing Sassy's a songstress was singing her blues: "I'm a bad woman. In the morning we fight and my man spanks my fanny till it hurts. But that's alright, honey. Cause when he comes home after a long day's work, he likes to pat and kiss my hurt. Yea, I'm a bad woman." Through the window you could see women standing to their feet and waiving their arms in air, swerving their hips and saying, “ouoooo,” before they sat down again. Patricia overheard her Granny mumbling, “What an awful and wicked song! They should be ashamed of themselves. Restaurant my foot, it’s nothing short of a beer garden and it should be closed down!” Very little ruffled Granny, but the words of that song seemed to. Patricia had heard the song several times before and liked the tune, but never really paid attention to the words until that evening.

Sassy didn’t attend church like her best friend Dottie, nor did she care for most of the people who did in Kendal Grove. Joe Carter was alright with her, since he was truly the only love of her life. He had even blessed her establishment before it reopened. She neglected to tell him at the time in addition to a restaurant, it was also a speakeasy. Yet, somehow Sassy felt he really knew her true intentions and blessed it just the same. His greeting remained the same to her at all times whether alone or in the presence of those self righteous church folk. Reverend Joe was a man, a real man, unlike any man she had known, and his son James was like him. Good men who married good women and that little Chaz will be like his daddy and his granddaddy. He too would be a godly man with a good woman to love him. She assured herself that she would apply the same rules to the little Carter man as she applied to his granddaddy and daddy. No woman that frequented her place would ever get close to them if she could help it. Nor would any nasty talk be said about them in her establishment. It was her place and her place meant her rules.

Sassy ran a tight ship. Still on occasion a fist fight or two might break out like the one Saturday night when Bouncy and Lucille got into it again over Lippy Johnson. “Miss. Sassy, Miss. Sassy!” Freckles yelled. “It’s Bouncy and she’s going to cut Lucille.” “Oh Lord!” Sassy yelped. “Why do those girls keep fighting over that man? Cause he don’t look like nothing with that big bottom lip and his skinny self. What happened?” “Bouncy was going to leave, but then she bent over, picked up a beer bottle and cracked it on a car fender, and went after Lucille." "Every time this kind of mess happens, it runs off my good customers. Bouncy! Put down that bottle, you ain't gonna cut nobody at my place! Now, what's the problem?" "She's trying to run off with my man!" Bouncy said pointing to Lucille. "Your Man?!" Lucille shot back, "He's mine and he's going home with me." "I'll put a stop to this right now! Lippy, which one of these gals you want going home with you?" Sassy asked. "Neither one of them is for me," Lippy replied. "I don't want nothing to do with no street fightin woman, no more. Look at them, looking a mess with their hair all over their heads, dirt on their faces and in their hair, stockings torn, and dresses ripped and falling off of them. I don't want anything to do with either one of them, no more." "There you have it," said Sassy. "He ain't going nowhere with either one of you. Go on home and fix yourselves up and stop acting like wild women. Lippy you get on out of here too. You should be out there helping your father on that cart."

Bouncy, Lucille and Lippy had no choice but to obey. If it had been any other woman they most likely would have bucked and turned on her. Sassy, not one to be trifled with, could have easily taken them on and beat each one of them within an inch of their lives. As Freckles put it, "She could still whip your ass quick, fast, and in a hurry, leaving you wondering. What happened?" She was a hefty, full figured, pretty lady with caramel skin, hazel eyes and shoulder length brown hair. Agile, yet getting on in age, she was not one you wanted to tangle with verbally or physically. Standing at five feet and eight inches she was as tall as most men and taller than others. Other than her height, girth and ability to handle herself in an altercation, she was all female. Who after working hours protected her feelings by virtually isolating herself from almost everybody in Kendal Grove. Neither her employees nor customers knew how sensitive she was and how easily she could be offended. Once called a "fruit cart" because of her fondness for white dresses with clustered fruit motifs, she cried for three days. Out to the trash went her collection of eight, printed summer dresses with clusters of apples, peaches, plumbs, grapes, strawberries, blue berries, pine apples and pairs.

Everyone knew she had a big heart by her treatment of the wine-o Freckles. William (Freckles) Canty was a bus driver. When he learned that several Negro children in the outlying areas could not make it to school because of the distance, a fund was started by Freckles to buy a used bus. After the bus was purchased he volunteered to drive the bus. He was one of the most upstanding residents in Kendal Grove until the bus accident in which fifteen people were killed, including Reverend Joe's wife, Althea and her parents, Lethea's father and Ricky's grandparents. The bus was returning from a revival when a car coming from the opposite direction turned sharply to avoid hitting a cow, in the middle of the road, and hit the bus head-on instead. The bus rolled over several times killing everyone inside except Freckles, who was driving the bus, and Reverend Joe. The driver of the car suffered a heart attack and died at the accident scene. Not at fault, he carried the blame for the others losing their lives and stayed drunk more than sober ever since. Freckles, was responsible for cleaning and keeping the grounds at Sassy's Place. Some thought he also provided other services for Sassy too. He wasn't just the handyman for her place, but also the handyman for her needs. Nevertheless, whether true or not Freckles was a permanent fixture at Sassy's Place and would continue to be.

Chapter Four
MISS. DOTTIE

A half mile down the dirt road that leads to the back of Sassy' place, in a little cottage, was where you could find the best homemade root beer, grape juice and a variety of baked goods. During the summer months on Wednesday afternoons Miss. Dottie's was the children's destination. Dottie was a dark, short and stout, white haired woman with a slender nose and thin lips. Who only put her teeth in and rolled her stockings up from around her ankles when she had adult company. Childless and widowed for over twenty years, she was respected and considered a no nonsense person and a good Christian. Unlike her ridiculously snobby and self righteous second cousins, the Chadwell sisters, she was caring. Extremely neat and well-disposed, she was also considered one of the best cooks in Kendal Grove. Having no dependable close male relatives to make repairs to the outside of her grayed, weather beaten home, it needed fixing up and her shambled outhouse too. The money she made from selling her pies, fruit cobblers, canned fruits, jellies and jams to the general store was only enough to buy the food she didn't grow herself, and pay the annual taxes on her land. Deemed so particular, the standard joke was that she didn't want birds to alight in her yard. Lenora, Chaz, Madeline and Ricky took pride in being allowed to visit with her, climb her fruit trees and play in her yard. Often on their visits Patricia would accompany them. Although, her house was thoroughly clean inside, Patricia often remarked how small it was and from the outside the only way you could distinguish the house from the outhouse was the house had windows.

Dottie loved visits from the children and watching them play in her yard. That is Lenora, Chaz, Ricky and Madeline. She was very fond of all children with the exception of one, Patricia. Not that she had any ill feelings toward anyone, but that child she would rather keep at a distance. Something wasn't right about Patricia. Lenora in contrast was quite the opposite. She was one child she could not get enough of and held a special place in her heart. After the children romped around Dottie's yard and finished their refreshments, they started off towards home with the exception of Lenora who stayed behind to help tidy-up and chat.

"You didn't know my husband Bert, he died a very longtime ago," Dottie said to Lenora after the other children had gone. "Sometime I sit here and pretend he is still with us, and we have a little girl who looks and acts like you. Lenora, I think the world of you and I believe everyone does, except that Hill girl. What's her name Patsy, Patty?" "No Miss. Dottie, I don't think Patricia doesn't like me, she is just that way." "Yea honey, only you would think that way because that's how you are. But let me tell you something, and I won't say nothing no more about it. That is a nasty little girl. I don't know why she is like that, her mother, God rest her soul, was a sweet one. But that little one is trouble, you hear what I say child? That one is lightening, thunder and a hail storm all rolled together wanting to strike somebody. You take care, because I think she is aiming straight at you."

Chapter Five
CAMP MEETING

August in Kendal Grove meant Camp Meeting-time. The theme, "The World Is a Beautiful Place with God in It," invigorated the residents of Kendal Grove. Invitation letters were sent to sister churches in the neighboring cities, counties and states. Collection envelopes were printed and distributed, as well as black and white posters mounted on telephone poles and trees all over Chrystol County announcing the event. As anticipated people came by the hundreds to worship and praise the Lord from as far east as New York and south as West Virginia on the second and third weekends during the last month of the summer. They also came to eat good food, visit with relatives, good friends, find a mate, and rekindle old flames. But the main objective for attending Camp Meeting was to hear the word of God and to sing his praises.

The closest hotels that catered to Negro people were located over sixty miles away in Washington D.C. or forty-five miles away in Parsons. Those who came to visit for Camp Meeting stayed with relatives, rented rooms, slept in their cars or camped outdoors under tents. The Carter and Howard households anticipated the arrival of Wendell and Marianne Heights to visit with them the second weekend in August. The "Six" as they referred to themselves growing up in Kendal Grove where one could never be found without the other. They hoped, dreamed and planned their futures together. James Carter would follow in his father's footsteps and become a preacher. Isaac Howard would continue to work for Mr. Tanner, a widower, with no children, who owned the general store. Learn the business, and acquire it within twelve to fifteen years of graduating high school and Wendell would teach. Not at the primary or high school levels, no, he wanted to become a college professor and teach at an institution of higher learning at a college or university. In order to reach his goal he studied profusely. Applied for and won scholarships based on his academic aptitude, and worked double shifts at odd jobs at his alma mater to receive his Undergraduate Degree. He furthered his education receiving his Masters Degree and finally his Doctorate of Philosophy. His diligence, humility, kindness and willingness to pass on the good he was bestowed to another won him countless awards and citations. Trusting in a higher power he was quoted as saying, "Whatever good you see in me comes from God. He surrounded me with good people during my upbringing who believed in me. I hope they would be proud of me, I guess I came out alright." Because of his once high ambitions his peers in Kendal Grove referred to him as "Highlife". Normally, he would have minded but those closest to him, Isaac, James, Lethea, Bertha and Marianne also referred to him as "Highlife". When they said it, they said it with dignity, as if it was a compliment and not a put down. The name stuck and after awhile the others began to say it in the same manner as his closest friends, and lifted their chins slightly as if they were giving a polite nod of approval. Each of the Six had their dreams, and all of their dreams had come to pass with the exception of the Heights' having children. Named godparents for both Chaz and Lenora, they loved them as if they were their own. Honk, honk, honk, sounded the horn of the automobile as it rolled under the outstretched branches of the massive oak tree in the Howard's driveway. Lenora and Chaz pushed open the screen door, ran down the front porch steps, down the walkway, across the yard and into Marianne's open arms. Marianne, excited to see the children, failed to notice that she was partially standing on the exposed roots of the oak tree that stood in the yard between the driveway and the house. Due to the impact of the children, she lost her balance and toppled over onto her knees. Highlife, retrieving their luggage from the trunk of the automobile, was unaware of the fall. If it was not for Lethea's scream, as she ran from the house to the aide of her friend, he would not have known that his wife had fallen and was bleeding from both knees. Despite the pain inflicted from the fall and her skinned knees, Marianne and the children were laughing hysterically. Realizing something was wrong when he heard the scream, Highlife dropped the bags, ran around to the front of the car, jumped over the log which separated the driveway from the front lawn and helped his wife to her feet. In his haste, he too almost toppled to the ground stumbling over the same tree roots where his wife lost her footing. He reached for his wife and godchildren, helping them regain their footing, than laughed at the former site of the three of them on the ground.

Isaac too, had reached them and asked, "Are you alright Marianne?" "Of course I am," she replied. "I'm here with my babies." "Your babies," said Lethea. "Your babies need a tanning. Apologize, you two for knocking over Marianne." "We are sorry Aunt M," said the children. "Oh, it's o.k. I am fine. It's not their fault, I got so excited that I forgot those old tree roots were there." "I apologize also," said Isaac. "I have got to do something about those roots. Lethea, take Marianne into the house and tend to her knees and I'll help Highlife with the bags." "I'm alright Isaac," said Marianne limping her way toward the house. "I'll be better though once I get some of Lethea's cake in me." "Only after I take a look at and fix those knees," said Lethea. "Look at your stockings, Marianne, beyond repair." "Always the mother, Lethea, always the mother," said Marianne hugging her friend rocking from side to side. "I heard Lethea scream and watched as she darted from the house, but I didn't see you coming Isaac," said Highlife. By-the-way, where were you?" "I was in the back fixing the shed when I heard your automobile pulling-up. The next thing I heard is Lethea screaming, than I see them sprawled all over the ground. Where was I, where were you? What were you doing? Is this some kind of new arrival ya'll learned in the big city? Pull up in a man's driveway, fall down, skin your knees and laugh?" Laughing, they debated over who would carry the luggage into the house. "Children run and tell Bertha and James that they're here," said Isaac. The children took off with joy toward Chaz's house. Not only were they glad it was Camp Meeting time but their godparents were in town and that meant presents.

Celebrating the Christian way of life in Kendal Grove at Camp Meeting was a festive occasion. Preparation was almost as important as the actual event. The men were assigned to refurbishing the grounds, repairing old wooden structures, or building new ones. Used as concession stands to sale food and cold beverages. Or they could be seen repairing and preparing the large wooden structure which served as the sanctuary for the welcomed guest. They were also detailed to transporting the food items from the houses of the best cooks in Kendal Grove to the campsite. The women cooked for days on end guarding their time proven creations from eager appetites for the weekend to come. They cooked and served for a small fee, collard and mustard greens, cabbage boiled with corn on the cob and seasoned with plenty of salted or smoked pork meat, fried chicken, pigs feet, chitterlings, old country ham, honey ham, turkey, rabbit, green beans, baked pork-n-beans, stewed tomatoes, macaroni and cheese, candied yams and sweet potatoes, boiled white potatoes, mashed potatoes and potato salad. They baked biscuits, rolls, cornbread, and lemon meringue, cherry, apple, sweet potato and peach pies, pound cake, and yellow cake with caramel, chocolate or coconut icing. Children anticipated this time of year for flavored ice, candied apples, homemade ice cream and great big slices of cake or pie. During Camp Meeting time children received unlimited freedom. The freedom was allowed as long as the adults were not disturbed, which seldom happened since they were obviously occupied with socializing and by the many church services provided. There was no limit on the fun the children could have and there was no limit on how much they could eat if they could afford it. To the children Camp Meeting was almost as good as Christmas morning and the only things missing were toys and the snow.

Young preachers and old alike looked forward to a chance to participate in the annual event. Receiving an invitation to speak at one of the services was considered an affirmation of the anointing of God, as well as one of the best preachers in the region to bring forth the word of God. Not to mention free meals of the best cooking for participating clergy. Reverend Joe kicked off the services with a fierce message: "Yes my brothers and my sisters, the Lord won't put on you more than you can bare, but Satan will try to brain ya. You see, brothers and sisters, I feel people confuse chastisement with punishment, misery and plain old torture. Now what kind of God would we serve if that's all there was to life? Life is a gift and it's a gift to be enjoyed. If you're not enjoying your life, if something is wrong – I mean always going wrong believe me when I say – it's not God in the midst! Call the enemy Satan, OUT! Rebuke him in the name of our Lord and Savior Jesus the Christ and Satan will have no choice but to flee! I say call him, OUT! Halleluiah, praise the holy name of Jesus! I say that the world is a better place with God in it. Do you hear me church? The world is a better place with God in it and I'm glad I know Him!"

The celebration not only brought those who thoroughly lived for the Lord, or who sought and found salvation in the Lord. It also brought those who needed salvation but wanted no part of it. The concession booths brought in a lot of money for the church and its social groups. The speakeasies and the gamblers also made a huge profit. Those looking for mischief could find it at the far end of the grounds, behind the shrubbery where a crap game could be found and the purse controlled by the bootleggers and moon shiners. When the goings-on were discovered at the far edge of the camp grounds was brought to the attention of Reverend Joe, he would fold his arms, take a deep breath and quote from the New Testament of the King James Bible, Romans 5:20 c-d: "But where sin abounded, grace did much more abound." Those in his entourage would nod in agreement and say, "Amen". Most of which were only too familiar with the goings-on. They too at one time had been a party to the same. Although, illegal activities were attended by a few at the far edges of the grounds, they were serenaded by the gospel singers and clergymen spouting the word of God. What Reverend Joe understood was subconsciously, they were still hearing the word of God. And God's word doesn't come back void.

Chapter Six
LETHEA'S BLESSINGS

Lethea loved Camp Meeting as everyone did in Kendal Grove. But the time had come which she least looked forward to, clean-up time once it was over. Her clean-up was relatively easy because her husband, Isaac, cleaned their kettle in which the candied-apple syrup was made. Volunteering to help others clean their six gallon kettles could sometime last for three days. As she sang hymns, cleaning the kettles, she praised God for indoor plumbing. Some people still had to haul water from the creek and some others from the well to wash their faces in the morning. She felt blessed to have indoor plumbing, hot and cold running water, as well as indoor toilets and a bathtub. Isaac Howard wouldn't have it any other way for his family. He promised to build her a house, if she agreed to marry him, and he did. Not any little old house, he built a nine room craftsman bungalow. With a large entry way, a built-in cherry mirrored wall tree with a bench and hat hooks, a living room, dining room, a big kitchen with a breakfast area and pantry, sewing room and little bathroom with a toilet and sink on the first floor; and on the second floor another bathroom with a bathtub and shower and three bedrooms. How she loved her God, her husband, her daughter, her family and friends. There could be no other woman in the world as happy, except for her best friend Bertha. We are the most blessed and happiest two women in the world, she thought. Everything in her life was fine and she would never want to be the cause of anything less. That's why she didn't mention to anyone the severe pain she had in her legs. Before Camp Meeting the pain was in the lower part of her left leg. Now the pain was in both legs and was so severe at times that it was all she could do not to scream. I've got so many things to do before I fix dinner, and I don't have time to think about the pain in my legs, she thought. "The geese will be flying south for the winter soon," she said to herself looking upward to the sky.

Chapter Seven
LENORA'S LEGACY

In the Howard household Monday was wash day. Lethea was more than grateful to have an electric washing machine which was similar to nothing she had seen before. "Live a life of leisure, no more wash tubs or scrub boards, sore knuckles or wringing clothes out by hand," the salesman said. And he was right. All she had to do was connect the long thick rubber hose of the machine to the kitchen faucet. Plug it in, put the dirty clothes into the machine, add detergent, and let the machine do the washing. Splashy, splash, gurgle, swish, splashy, splash, gurgle, swish, went the machine. Lethea chuckled as she watched the washing machine take on a personality of its own, dancing in place on the back porch. When the dancing stopped it was time to prepare the wet clothes for wringing. Pulling the clothes through the built-in wringer before hanging them out to dry, cut her washing time in half. It sure beat the way she used to wash. There was not a woman in Kendal Grove who would dispute that claim, she thought, taking her wash out to dry in the crisp morning air.

As she began to hang her wash on the line piece by piece, holding the garments in place on the clothes line with wooden clothes pins she took from her apron pocket, she wondered what Lenora was doing in school. Her baby had recently begun the forth grade. Time really goes by fast, and before you know it she will be out of school and teaching. She hoped Lenora would marry Chaz and have a family. Lethea couldn't think of anyone else in the world other than Bertha to share her grandchildren with. They could build their home on the land her daddy left them right next to their home. Her life will be great, like hers. The sky began to cloud over and it was getting darker by the second. I really don't like when it rains on my wash, she thought.

Lenora arrived home from school with her father waiting at the front gate. "Hi daddy," she said returning her fathers embrace. "Why are you here? Where is mother?" Lenora was not familiar with the expression shown on her daddy's face. "What is it, daddy?" she asked. He took her hand in his and walked silently towards the house. Knowing something was terribly wrong, and unable to persuade her father to speak, Lenora sat quietly on the front porch next to him awaiting a reply to her question. "It's your Mother, Sweetie," he said softly, holding back his tears. "What's wrong with mother, daddy, where is she?" "She is upstairs in our bedroom, Dr. Mitchell is with her." At that moment Chaz and his parents were coming through the front gate. Bertha ran up to Isaac, lifted his face to her face. "Tell me she is alright," she said. "Please tell me she is alright, Isaac!" There was no reply from Isaac. James took hold of his inconsolable wife and pulled her close to him. Isaac lowered his head again and covered his face with his hands. Lenora and Chaz stared at one another in bewilderment. "I've got to go to her, I have got to go to her," Bertha cried. "Wait." James said softly, as he tried to console his wife. "Let's wait to see what the doctor has to say." Breaking away from James' hold, Bertha grabbed Lenora and held her tight. Lenora could not remember ever being held so tight. She could sense that something was wrong with her mother. That had to be the reason for her daddy crying and Aunt Bertha actions. She looked at her daddy, at her Uncle James, at Chaz and at her daddy again. The doctor partially opening the screen door motioned for Isaac to enter the house. Lenora could see her father sitting on the window seat through the living room window, the doctor sitting down next to him. She could not hear what was being said, but she could tell that her father was taking in every word the doctor was saying. As if it were the first time he had heard a voice. The doctor's mouth stopped moving, he arose and walked away from where her father was left sitting. The only person in view was her father with his eye's fixed in the same position as when the doctor was seated next to him. Doctor Franklin leaving quietly through the front door softly shut the screen door behind him. Stooping down in front of Lenora, he said, "No one will ever love you like your mother and father. You mean everything to both of them and no matter what happens from this day forward never forget that." He gently brushed her cheek with the back of his hand and walked towards James. Placing his hand upon James' shoulder, the doctor said, "He is your best friend and you have to be there for him." "What's wrong?" asked James. "Blood clots, she didn't tell anyone about the pain in her legs and now it's too late to do anything to save her life." Bertha gripping the front door frame as if she were trying to become a part of the house, turned away from the doctor as he walked toward her. Placing his hand on her back, the doctor said, "Lethea wants to see you." "I can't!" Bertha cried. "You have to, if you don't Bertha, you will never forgive yourself." "Doctor, I can't imagine life without her." "You will have to Bertha, life goes on and we go with it. Hold on to your memories and she'll be with you." The doctor, leaving, turned to James and said, "I will find your father and send him over." "Thank you," said James holding his wife in his arms. Lenora, looking through the window, watched her father stand to his feet. Despondent, Isaac, rubbed his hands over his head and face, and gathered his thoughts. He needed to concentrate on comforting his little girl. After straightening his jacket, he partially opened the screen door and held his hand out for his daughter, and said, "Let's go see your momma, she is waiting for us." Lenora could barely lift her feet to meet each step. Through the railing she could see the white lace curtains, the ones her grandmother sent from New York, in her parent's bedroom lift to the cool breeze coming through the window. Reaching the top landing, Lenora held her breath still unaware of what was happening to her mother.

Her father sat on the edge of their bed taking her mother's hand into his hand. He whispered to Lethea, "Our baby is here." "Oh." She said, opening her eyes to search for Lenora. "My baby is home from school, where?" "Yes momma, I am here." "Come hug me Lenora, I won't break. Come hug me real tight like you do when you come home from school. Sit here." She patted the space on the bed between her and Isaac. "Lay up here beside momma and daddy."

"Momma, what's wrong? What happened to you, why are you in bed?" Lenora asked. "Don't ask so many questions baby," said Isaac. "It is alright." Lethea said, holding her daughter in her arms. "I am not well, Lenora. I haven't been for a while and I never told anyone, so remember, this is no ones fault. I am a happy woman with happy thoughts who has been blessed with people who have only brought joy and happiness into my life. Look at you, look at your daddy, look at my friends and look at my surroundings. I am truly grateful to my Lord and Savior for everything. So it's fine for me to go home to be with my Father in heaven. It's alright for me to go be with the Lord." Lenora was not sure what her mother was saying. When people wanted to be with the Lord they went church. Puzzled, Lenora looked to her father for answers who was crying. At the bedroom door stood Chaz and his parents. "Come on in my little prince," said Lethea. Chaz, with his parents entered the bedroom and stood on the opposite side of the bed from Lenora and her father. Lenora, perched-up on one arm, prone alongside her mother, watched Chaz sit down on the bed next to her mother. "If I had a little boy, I would have hoped for him to be exactly like you. Love your parents as they love you and from time to time remind Lenora of how much I love her." Chaz, listening and retaining what he was hearing, was unable to understand why his Aunt Lethea was speaking in this manner. He nodded in agreement. Bertha unable to maintain her emotions any longer dropped to her knees at the bedside of her best friend. She asked, "Why didn't you tell me you were in pain? You tell me everything." "I didn't want to worry you." "Worry me?" "You have never done anything in your life to worry me." "I know, and I didn't want to start now. Bertha, you know, the hand painted scarf you love so much that my mother sent me for Christmas?" "Yes." Bertha replied. "I want you to have it, and make sure you wear it on Home Coming Sunday. I was going to let you wear it then anyway." With her strength rapidly waning Lethea held Lenora's face in her hands. Before kissing her cheek she whispered, "Love and put God first, love your husband and your children, and make sure your daddy is alright. All that I have is yours.

You are my beautiful little lady and a good girl. I've prayed that you will have a wonderful life according to the will of God."

As the dry leaves of autumn softly tumbled away with the evening breeze so did Lethea pass away to be with the Lord on that September evening. "I wish my mother was here," were Lethea's last spoken words.

Chapter Eight
FAREWELL

There was a line of people that extended all the way around the church to view Lethea's body and pay their last respects. Lenora had no idea her mother and father knew so many people, and had never seen the church filled past its capacity. Lenora heard countless times, "My, how beautiful she is" and "She was a wonderful woman," as people passed by her and her father seated on the front pew. Her grandmother Helen and Aunt Agnes were also sitting on the pew beside her. Those on the pew behind her were great aunts and uncles, cousins and other relatives that she didn't know. It was strange to see her Godfather, Highlife, and his wife her Godmother, Marianne, so soon after Camp Meeting time. Although, she was sitting with her daddy's arm around her, as well as surrounded by relatives and friends who truly loved her, she only wished her mother could say something to her. She wanted so badly to let Lethea know that her mother had come. She wanted to look two pews back to her right to see her mother sitting in the place where she sat every Sunday. Who would sit in her mother's place on Sunday? She thought. Deep within her little heart she knew that her mother was in a much better place, and what she saw was only a shell. That she learned in Sunday school but she couldn't help wanting her mother alive and well, laughing and talking with their family members and friends.

Chaz and Ricky waived at Lenora as they passed by her to view her mother's body. Lenora was surprised to see Mr. Macabee, Ricky's father, enter the church, something she had surely never seen before. Then she noticed Ricky was a miniature version of his father except his father had a thin mustache. They had the same build, light brown completion, curly, sandy brown hair, light brown eyes, well-defined noses, pursed lips and strong chins. She watched Macabee intensely as he viewed her mother. Turning away from the casket, with his hat in his left hand, he extended his right hand to greet her father. "I am sorry for your loss," he said in his smooth and mellow voice. "She was a good woman." "Thank you, yes she was," said Isaac, nodding in agreement.

The funeral wasn't very long thought Lenora even though three hours had past since she last looked at the time. She waved good-bye and blew a kiss to her mother's casket as they lowered it into the grave. As her grandmother and aunt led her away from the gravesite she saw her father standing motionless, starring into her open grave. Not knowing what to do Lenora held tightly to her grandmother's hand as they walked toward the car for the ride home. Still unable to grasp the reality of his wife's passing, Isaac continued to stare into the grave. Not because he was saying "good-bye" to the only woman he had ever loved, he thought a cruel joke had been played on him. And at any second Lethea would appear from somewhere, anywhere, and go home with him and Lenora. "It's time to go," said James. "Yes, I know," said Isaac. Throughout this whole thing, I kept thinking she would appear from anywhere. I guess that's foolishness, huh?" "Foolishness, not you Isaac, you are the most level headed man I know. You are only looking for answers to something you can't understand. It was easier for you to think she would appear than accepting the fact that she is no longer with us in the flesh. No that is not foolishness, your heart is heavy and you want to make sense of it all." "Tell me this Preacher-man, what have I done to make God so angry with me? Why, would He take the only thing on this earth I have ever loved?" "God didn't take everything you ever loved. You still have Lenora, your business, your health, and you know you have me and my family. Personally Store-boy, I don't think that God took her as a punishment to us. It was her time to go be with the Lord. It is not of God to cause misery to the righteous. Pain, confusion and broken heartedness are weapons of the enemy. The Holy Scripture tells us that our God is a healer of the broken hearted, down trodden and oppressed. Call on the Lord my brother he will have all of the answers. The reading of God's word and prayer in the throne room of grace will give you the answers to all of your questions. When you are ready, and only when you are ready, God will reveal the answers to you. I'll send everyone else to the house and you can ride with me." The two friends rode together silently to the repast.

As they parked in front of the Howard's home, Isaac half-heartedly looked at his beautiful home. He realized Lethea would never again welcome him home. "She is gone, James," said Isaac." "Yes she is," said James. "She has gone home to be with our Lord." "I can imagine heaven to be a better place with her, Preacher-boy. I mean, she was so good at loving us. Think about the joy she must have felt when she met the Lord." They smiled imagining Lethea meeting the Lord. "Do you think she changed the bed linens yet, James?" "Isaac, if heaven has bed linens, you know she did." They chuckled at the thought before joining the others at the repast.

Chapter Nine
BERTHA'S FRIEND

Following the passing of Lethea, her nearest and dearest friend, Bertha had almost lost her will to live. After finishing her chores the remainder of her day was spent in bed. There was no one to express her thoughts or feelings to but God. Everyday, for three months she repeated the same prayer before drifting off to sleep: "Oh my Father, I know you loved her more than I could ever imagine, but I miss my friend. I miss her kindness, her fondness for life and the love she had for you. Ease my pain, Father. I know you are with me. In the name of your precious son, Jesus the Christ, I pray. It is so."

Little seven year old Annie Potts was the answer to Bertha's prayers. The youngest of the nine children of Thomas and Beulah Potts, was a site to see. She was a little yellow skinned girl that sucked her two middle fingers and had plats that weren't long enough to meet sticking up all over her head. Although clean, her tattered hand-me down baggy clothes fit her like a circus clown's costume. She had the sweetest disposition and a visit from Annie was the only thing other than a visit from Lenora that could bring a smile to Bertha's face. Initially, meant to be a temporary arrangement, Annie began spending entire weeks with the Carter family to help ease the pain of Bertha's loss. On weekends she would return home with her family to Picker's Woods. Bertha was often overheard saying, "She didn't know what she would have done after the passing of her best friend, if it had not been for Annie."

The Potts were hard working tobacco sharecroppers, who as many families found it not easy to make ends meet. Alongside their six boys and two other daughters they worked sharecropping a fourteen acres parcel on one of the largest farms in the county. Burrell was the eldest than Cutta, Harvey, Ethel, Irwin, Kate, Phillip, Alec and Annie. None could read or write and they spoke an idiom of gibberish that was only spoken and understood, on the most part, by the Pickers. Shabby, as they may be and uncoordinatedly clad, the children were polite and the entire family attended Sunday school and church services. When the Carter's asked if Annie could live with them and be treated as their child, the Potts agreed to deliberate on it for a day or so before giving an answer.

The wagon ride to their shack from church was no different from any other except that they had a major decision to make concerning one of their children. "Wha you think, Ma?" asked Thomas. "I not real sho Pa," answered Beulah. "Most we know lose to, tree chulin befo dae fo or fie yer ole. She ete, but it ain't lik Annie do no whol lot work in de feil, no how." "No Ma, dat gal Ethel kin pic and hal as much as eny man. Kate ain't to bad eiver. She don do much as Ethel but se kin hal er own. But dat lil Annie she ain't goin to mount to much workin wif us in de fiels pickin. Maybees da teech her how to read n write and talk like da does? Dat Miss. Berfa really crazy bout dat lil gal. Ya no Ma, we been blessed. I did pect to lose one or two chulin to def, but I nev pect to lose one to the livin." "I figua you den made up your min den." "Yes sah, I have – lil Miss. Annie tis goin to live in de Preacha's house wit de rich folk." Annie wanted to live with the Carters but was going to sorely miss the closeness of her Mother, her eldest brother, Burrell, and her sister, Ethel. Her bother Burrell despite his large size was the most gentle and kind man she knew. He loved animals and was most gentle with the smaller ones. Annie once found a baby bird that had fallen from its nest after a heavy down pour. She scooped up the helpless bird and rushed it home. Not knowing what to do she asked her siblings advice on caring for the chirping baby bird. None gave the bird a second thought except for Burrell. He carefully checked the bird for broken bones with his massive hands. Finding none he took some hey from his parent's bed and shreds of material. He than placed the bird in the nest made of hey and gently surrounded it with the material torn from his shirt. His next steps proved to be a great hunting expedition for Annie. They went a short distance from their shack to dig up worms for the baby bird to eat. With the gentleness of a caring country doctor, Burrell helped Annie nurse the orphaned bird until it was strong enough to fly off on its own.

Ethel, her eldest sister, was a big girl in every way including her heart. She was a quick study and as she grew older became open to things that would increase her knowledge and enhance her surroundings. The enhancement of her appearance came upon her quite suddenly. From the first time she saw the home of the Carter's she took stock in the colossal difference in their living arrangements and her own. Ethel wanted the best for herself and her family. Possessing a stellar work ethic, her interest in picking and hauling with the strength of a boy her age, was wearing thin. At sixteen she no longer wanted to be compared to boys. She was a girl, a young woman and despite her size wanted to be treated as such. There wasn't much pleasure in a Picker's life. No dumb Picker, she also noticed that there was a difference in speech and in the mannerisms of the residents, the Hill people and the pickers. She was conscious of Pickers feeling lowly, acting as such and ultimately treated as such. She was also conscious that they shied away from education and the better things in life, as if they were undeserving. They were a people who worked like mules all their lives and expected nothing in return. That is why she specifically asked to escort her little sister the eight miles from their shack to the Carter's. Ethel was more than thrilled the chance finally came her way to get a look at the interior of the preacher's home.

There were no kisses, hugs or long good-byes the morning Annie left the Pott's shack to go live with the Carter's. Beulah removed the burlap potato sack from the clothesline she had washed the night before. In it she packed her little girl's dress, two undershirts, one pair of socks and a pair of under bloomers. The other dress, pair of under bloomers and socks Annie had on. Her mother handed her the burlap sack, and her father lifted her into the homemade wagon. "Be a goot lil gal," her mother said. Ethel took hold of the wagon handle and led her little sister toward her new home. The eight mile walk was nothing to Ethel as she pondered the many sites she would behold entering the Preacher's, Victorian, house. Ethel took in every detail as they approached their destination. There was no debris or junk anywhere in their yard. No old broken buckets, or barrels, broken tools, rags, ash cans, trash or anything of that nature around the house. They had two feet tall stone walls on each side of the three feet wide by twelve feet long flagstone walkway. Four stone steps led to a wooden porch, and two white columns stood on either side of the steps supporting the porch roof. And two of the biggest and cleanest windows she had ever seen were at each side of the double front doors. With Annie by her side she cautiously walked up the stone steps onto the porch. When they approached the double doors, with her little hand balled into a fist, Annie knocked twice, opened one of the doors and walked into the vestibule. Is this the inside of the house? Ethel thought, sizing up the space in the vestibule. The house looked a whole lot bigger to her from outside. As Annie closed the doors behind them, she noticed another set of double doors, half colored glass and half wood. Ethel reached out to touch the glass, as Reverend James Carter opened the vestibule doors from the other side and said, "Hello Ethel. Welcome. Why you and Annie come on in and have a seat." She was inside and what she beheld was breathtaking. The room was a glow due to the bright sunlight shimmering through the windows. There was no dust anywhere, everything was fresh and clean. The colors in the coordinated tapestries seemed to dance in the afternoon sunlight. The house smelled of cinnamon and cherry pipe tobacco. Each room was lavishly furnished, and accented with vases, crystal candy dishes and ash trays, doilies and table covers, and hanging pictures on the walls. They even had a piano. "Is that Annie?" Bertha asked entering the front hall from the kitchen while wiping her hands on her apron. "Yes, it's me," said Annie. Bertha got down on one knee to hug Annie, and said, "Welcome home, you little precious thing." James took Annie's bag and dropped it into a corner, hoisted her into his arms and gave her a tremendous hug. "Are you ready to show Ethel your bedroom?" he asked. "Yes sir," said Annie.

"Let's go to it, you lead the way," he said as he gently put Annie down. Annie took Ethel's hand and led her around the staircase and down the hall. "Haw many rooms dis house have?! Ethel said to herself. "Wha is a bedroom, and ware do does steps go?" she also said to herself. Annie led Ethel to the room adjacent to James' study which she thought was her bedroom. To her surprise all of Reverend Joe's things were in her room. "Isn't this my room?" asked Annie. "No it isn't," Bertha replied. "You're going to be upstairs with us. You'll have the room next to Chaz's." Ethel was still unable to utter a sound. Not for fear of being made fun of because of the ridicule Pickers receive from the residents when they spoke. She was mum from her amazement of the size and beauty of the house. Ethel followed her sister upstairs without saying a word. Upstairs Ethel saw four more rooms, and could no longer hold her silence. "Wha dees room fo?" she asked. "There are three to sleep in and one to bathe in," said Annie. "Wha?" Annie showed the other rooms to Ethel. She clicked on the electric light switch in each room to illuminate its contents. Annie's room was wonderful. She had her own bed with a mattress, sheets and a blanket. A few hours ago, Annie was asleep on hey, under an old horse blanket, between her two sisters, across the room from her parents on their bed of hey and horse blankets. Her brothers were asleep on the front porch in piles of leaves and hey. During the colder months they came inside and slept on the floor. That's when quarters became too close with them spread out over the floor. Annie had a dresser, a nightstand and two electric lamps. Lace curtains at her windows and window shades, a rug and two pillows, a chair and a clothes closet. Clothes were in her closet; a coat and two new pairs of shoes, and in her tissue paper lined drawers she had more clothes and undergarments. Ethel asked, "Ware de outhouse?" "There is no outhouse, Ethel," said Annie. "Follow me. We use this, a toilet," Annie said pulling the cord to flush. "Ware dat wator go, don ya'll drink dat?" "No, toilet water is dirty water. We drink water from the faucet downstairs in the kitchen. But we can drink this water too. That's what this little glass is for, see." Annie pointed to the glass, on the self above the bathroom sink, than demonstrated how the faucets worked before going back downstairs.

From what Ethel could fathom her little sister was about to live the good life. And with Ethel's compassionate heart she couldn't be happier for her. Asked to stay for tea, Ethel happily accepted the offer to spend more time basking in lavishness. Her mind was spinning with new revelations as she slurped her tea and ate her tea cakes. She must learn how to read, write and speak right, because this is the life for her. Her mind than reeled back to what the visiting preacher said a few weeks prior: "If you want to make a change in your life you must start today!" he shouted. Tomorrow is not promised! Life is a gift!" Someday, she was going to build her own house and have pretty things too. Annie nudged her sister, concluding her reverie, saying, "Don't slurp your tea like that. Sip it quietly like this." Ethel again followed her baby sister's lead, as they drank tea and ate tea cakes, together with the Carter's, in Annie's new home.

Eight years old to fourteen years old seemed to take place overnight to Bertha. Her little Annie was now a blossoming young woman. And she had a nerve to have a little boy friend, her sister Ethel's fiancé's helper, Sonny. "He's a cute little old curly head thing too with his broad shoulder and quick stride. A nice young fellow being raised by the Case's over in Parsons. He thinks he's a grown man at seventeen," Bertha said talking to herself. Bertha could go on for days, while doing her chores, laughing and talking, and having conversations with self. When they were first married James asked, "How in the world can you hold conversations with yourself so much?" She answered, "It makes the day go by faster." His response was simply, "Oh." He figured, if it made her happy and she could come up with an answer that fast, and worked for her, let it be. "That's pretty," she said putting the last bit of pink icing on the double layer angel food cake. Annie walked into the kitchen and asked, "Why pink?" "I can't rightly say, Annie. I guess I wanted something different. By-the-way, Brother Dan will be having supper with us tonight." "Oh my Lord, the black praying mantis will be following me wherever I go for the entire evening as usual," Annie said silently to herself. Bertha watched Annie's shoulders droop and her countenance change. "Don't worry darling, I'll try to distract his attentions from you tonight. There is some mission work I'd like to discuss with him this evening. Being a preacher means more than eating dinner at the Senior Pastor's house and making every attempt possible to get the attention of his daughter." "Thank you Momma Bertha, thank you. Sonny is coming by tonight and he would like to have a talk with all of you. That is you and the Reverends, not Brother Dan." "That's fine with me, Sweet Darling. We'll all talk when he gets here."

Brother Dan was born and raised in Pickers Woods and was the closest thing that the Pickers had to a clergy. His designs were set on marrying Annie since she was also from beyond the Hill. He was a tall, skinny and dark man with a long, crooked nose and a gruesome grin which shown his black gums and yellow teeth. He wore spectacles that set on the edge of his nose, which he believed gave him a worldly and sophisticated look. He had a long skinny neck and his arms and legs were to long for his torso. His suits never fit him properly and when Bertha politely asked to let down his jackets and trousers, he flatly refused. He than said in an arrogant snarl, "Madam, I prefer my suits to fit me this way. I appreciate your interest, just the same." She nodded and politely smiled in total contrast to what she was thinking or feeling. He knew his bible and he could preach the word, but something didn't add-up about him. In honest he didn't set well with the Reverends. They hoped and prayed his liturgical demeanor was a true calling from God and not an act to warrant undue reverence. So he was often invited by the Carters to supper and on spiritual outings in support of his calling. But his blatant cooing for Annie was about to put an end to all of his invitations. To Brother Dan's dismay, directly after dessert he was asked to be pardoned because family business needed to be discussed. His dismay turned into sheer rage when as he was exiting the front gate Sonny was entering into it. When Sonny knocked at the door, he was ushered in. With angst Brother Dan walked all the way home to Pickers Woods that evening at a fevered pace.

"She has to quit school because of her condition," Sonny said pausing and clearing his throat before he continued. "I was hoping she could stay on with you, after we are married, and work as a housekeeper. I am out on the road two to three months at a time. Right now I am a driver's helper and I'm saving for my own truck. I've been working steady for almost two years, ever since I graduated high school." Taken aback with the news Sonny had brought them, James, Bertha and Joe, saddened, bowed their heads. Before they could asked any questions Sonny said, "I'm hoping you'll marry us this weekend, Reverend Joe. I am due on the road again Wednesday of next week and won't be back for awhile." Still there was no answer. Uncustomary, because everyone in the household was a quick thinker and could respond to any question before you could blink an eye. Annie searched what little she could see of Bertha's face for a hint of a smile. There was no expression whatsoever on her face. Then finally came a response from James, saying, "Annie you and Sonny go on outside. Take a walk for a half-hour or so and then come back." The closing of the front door gave way to full animation. "What's wrong with this family," asked James? "Poppa you have to stop stomping, huffing and puffing, and Bertha you have to stop crying." "What's wrong daddy?" asked Chaz as he came through the front door. "Annie is having a baby," his father answered. "Who's the father?" "What do you mean, who is the father!" Joe shouted. "What are you saying about our little Annie?" "No, Grand Poppa, I didn't mean it that way. I was surprised by the news that's all. I know it has to be Sonny." Bertha had only seen her father-in-law madder than a hatter once before and that was about fifteen years ago when Mavis Stone, Ricky's mother, was hospitalized. The huffing and puffing, foot stomping and banging his fist into his hand went on for an entire night. On their return into the house composures had been regained, and it was time to move forward. "Sonny, Annie is like our own little girl, but we are not her people," said James. "The permission for her hand should come from her father. You do know her father, who he is?" "No sir, I can't rightly say that I do," Sonny replied. "I didn't think so," said Joe removing his pipe from his mouth. He turned it over and emptied its contents of spent tobacco into the ash tray, and then reassured his daughter-in-law by gently patting her shoulder. Both James and Bertha sat motionless, as Joe probed Sonny and paced the study floor. Annie too sat like a little lady, motionless, unable to look anyone in the eye. "Well son, I guess we should get ready to take this boy up the way," said Joe. "Alright, Poppa," said James, "do you think we'll need any guns?" "No, I think we'll be alright, they know the car," Joe said stuffing his pipe with fresh cherry tobacco. Sonny, standing in the middle of the floor with his cap in hand didn't know what to think. "Guns, why would we need guns?" Sonny asked. "Because we going into some dangerous territory," Joe answered. "Let us do the talking, and when it's your turn to talk we'll let you know. You most likely won't understand a word they're saying. Listen hea, after awhile you might catch a bit of what they're saying. Still, don't open your mouth until one of us tells you it's alright to do so." "Do you understand Sonny?" asked James. "Yes sir, I do." "Then let's get on our way." "Be careful said Bertha," as she waived from the front door. Her husband and father-in-law drove off with Annie's intended, the father of her unborn child. Bertha still couldn't utter a word to Annie. "So this is why Sonny wanted to speak with us this evening," Bertha said to herself. "Oh Lord, please don't let Mr. Potts or Annie brothers kill that boy," she quietly prayed.

"Did you get the matches, son?" Joe asked James. "Yes Poppa," responded James. "Where the heck are they taking me," Sonny said to himself. "We're in a dense wooded area miles past the Hill. I was told that the Hill people were the roughest and meanest people you could run into around these parts. Wherever we're going the people must be worse. "Where are we going," asked Sonny? "To a place called, Pickers Woods," said James. "Why is it that I've never heard of it?" "It's because you're not from around here, and you're not a Picker. You haven't met anyone from there other than Annie, Ethel and Brother Dan, and they don't talk about Picker's Woods or what goes on there." "Sir, do you mean pickers as in sharecroppers and people who work on farms and in orchards?" "Yes." You hit the nail right on the head," said Joe. "Is that all?" Sonny said smiling and sliding back into the comfort of his seat. "Is that all!" the two men in the front seat said in unison. They then looked at each other and chuckled. James looked through the rearview mirror at Sonny and Joe over his left shoulder. The following words hit Sonny like a jack hammer. "Let me tell you something young fellow, if we didn't truly worship and love the Lord we'd let you out right here on the side of this road and leave you," said Joe. If we did that we both might as well be charged with murder, and Annie would give birth to her child with no father. You see, we have to keep you alive, first because we're real Christian men and we have to answer to the Lord. Second, we really love our Annie, so we can't leave you out here alone to die. These people, in Picker's Woods, have their own language and their own set of laws, rules and regulations. There are only a handful of them that come to church, go to school, shop at Howard's store or socialize with the people on the Hill. It's silly, but they're practically barred from associating with the residents of Kendal Grove. They're what one could consider an independent civilization. They don't bother us and we don't bother them."

James than turned off the highway onto an unnoticeable, rutted, dirt wagon wheel road. Ump, ump the car grunted as it tilted one way then the other. "Watch it now, son," said Joe. "Make sure you stay as best you can in those wagon wheel tracks. "I've got it, Poppa," said James. Grreer, grreer, the gear shift echoed in the darkness. It was pitch black in the woods and the head lamps made little difference. About a half-mile down the rutted road Joe said, "Alright, put a stop to it right here, James." "Why are we stopping?" asked Sonny. He was beginning to feel uneasy in the eerie darkness. Something was very strange about the entire situation, and he didn't like it. Then there they were all of a sudden. Two men with shot guns – both the same color as the night and the double barrel shot guns they were holding.

It was only the moonlight that briefly shown through the clouds that revealed the watchmen of Pickers Woods. "That you Pooka," asked Joe? "Ya, who u?" the old grey haired, leather faced, toothless man shot back. It was then that James stuck a match in the car. "Et u Precha-man?" "Yea, and son plus this boy here." The two men extended their arms and shook at each others elbows. "Ain't see u fo a bit o time, Precha. It goot see u and son. Wa too?" "Potts," answered Joe. "K, let em gooo," the old man shouted as he lifted his right arm over his head. Sonny than heard and saw the strangest thing he could ever imagine. On the other side of the car in the darkness were four other men also holding shotguns. He could also make out the outline of a makeshift dwelling of some sort. Than came some short of call, "Yawoo, Preacha-man, son plus one comin – Potts." It was about one quarter of a mile when he heard another call. This time it came from a woman and there was no sign of her. She hollered, "ya'll" instead of "yawoo." Then again in the darkness there appeared the makings of what could be a house. They passed Brother Dan standing at the edge of the road in the foreground of what must be his house, which resembled an expanded outhouse with a front porch. The only way they knew he was standing at the edge of the road was because of the long draw from the pipe he was smoking illuminated his face. He nodded as they passed wondering what business they could be calling about at this hour of the night in Picker's Woods. Why wasn't he consulted, leaving the home of the Carter's less than two hours ago? He thought. Sonny heard two more calls before they stopped. Then he heard what he thought was the confirmation that they had reached their destination. "Heraaa – Preacha-man, son plus one!" The dusty, old man with a stocky build responded to the night calls, standing on his front porch smoking a corn cob pipe. His clothes were old and worn and his pockets on both his shirt and pants were frayed, and the hem of his pants had been let down. His shoes, although, clean were worn and the soles were visibly coming apart. His face was clean shaven and his hair was neatly combed, and he still looked dusty. Sonny came to the conclusion that the unknown man was surely an oddity and came right out of the funny papers. He decided as with all of his elders, this man too would be treated with respect. He had no idea the man was his future father-in-law.

The Potts took the news calmly. Annie was of marrying age and the young man was going to marry her. He wasn't a bad looking young fellow, plus he had a real good job. They were happy with the knowledge of Annie going to have it better than any Picker's Woods girl ever had it before. They believed that their Annie was special and they were pleased to know that others felt the same.

The next morning brought both hustle and bustle to the Carter house. It was only four days before Annie's wedding on Saturday and there was much to do. Concluding morning prayers with her husband, James, Bertha was off to make a list for what needed to be done. There was no time for a real house cleaning, so a quick spruce had to do. For which wasn't necessary in her immaculately kept home. "Let's see, wedding dress, bridesmaids' dress, bouquets, refreshments, oh yes, and how can I forget the wedding cake," said Bertha. "James, don't forget to remind Daddy to call the Cases." "Yes dear," he replied. "Annie wedding dress was an easy fix. The top of her off white lace Easter dress and the bottom of her cream, satin Spring Ball dress would make a nice wedding dress. What a coincidence the two dresses combined would fit the occasion, because it was out of the question for her to wear white. I know I can count on Dottie for the bouquets and flower arrangements and both Lenora and Madeline will help in anyway they can. Now the bridesmaid, oh my goodness, she'll need dress, shoes and her hair done. Goodness gracious that will be Lenora's and Madeline's assignment. I remember the first time I tried to do Annie's hair. I didn't know a light skinned girl could have such nappy hair. Ethel had buck shot naps and that was bad enough. Annie's naps were smaller than bee bees and more like roe. It took Dottie and her hair grease and twine to train that girl's hair. If my memory serves me correctly, Aunt Molly's old trunk is up in the attic. She was a big woman, not as big as Ethel. With a snip here and there to let out the seams...that might work. Are you listening, James?" "Yes dear," he replied.

After breakfast clean-up the Carter men, the youngest to the eldest, swiftly sought refuge at the church from the commotion at home. It was 11:00AM when Dottie, Lenora and Madeline arrived to receive their assignments from Bertha. "Do you want a one or two layer wedding cake?" asked Dottie. "Two layers would do nicely Miss. Dottie," said Annie. "If it was a summer wedding my white roses and azaleas would be just right for your bouquets, and decoration for the top of the cake. Instead I'll make sugar flowers for the cake and use ribbons for the bouquets." "That's a great idea, Dottie," said Bertha. "I've never been introduced to your sister," said Lenora, "what is she like?" Annie smiled as she described her sister. Bertha chimed in, "wait until you see her again. Ethel has become quite the pretty girl since moving to Parsons. She is a darling and you'll love her." Bertha remembered when she scrubbed Ethel from head to toe. It took gobs and gobs of her homemade face and hand cream to reach any sort of gleam in her skin. Her hair, fingernails and feet were atrocious and required rigorous scrubbing. The poor child didn't know her measurements, dress or shoe size. Bertha smiled the self-assuring smile she was known for, before returning her thoughts back to the planning of Annie's wedding. "I have only one pair of silk stockings and those go to Annie for her special day." "Thank you, Momma Bertha," said Annie.

It was October and several of the ration tickets being saved for Thanksgiving dinner were used. As a token of love and support for Annie the Howard's and the Trusdale's presented a gift of ration tickets for the wedding party. With the extra tickets, Bertha and Annie planned and prepared a sumptuous wedding feast. There were twelve place settings at the beautifully decorated dinner table. They served minced cheese finger sandwiches, butter pickles, peanuts and dainty peppermints for advertisers. The soup was onion and the entree included both roast beef and ham with mashed potato's, pickled beets with onions, peas with mushrooms and hot buttered rolls. Dottie outdid herself with the wedding cake. The sugar roses and azalea flowers adorning the cake looked fresh picked. Sonny was extremely nervous and was grateful for his best man Ben, and Chaz to lend him support. He didn't know that the Cases, Daddy Earl and Momma Estelle, knew the Carters the Howard's, the Trusdale's and Miss. Dottie. Until that day he had never met Madeline Trousdale or her parents or Miss. Dottie for that matter. He knew Lenora and Mr. Howard from making frequent deliveries to the store. Clearly not present was Annie's family except for her big sister Ethel who stood as her bridesmaid. The ceremony performed by Reverend Joe was appropriate, short and simple. The third Saturday in October, despite the premature occasion of Annie's pregnancy and marriage, brought much gaiety to the Carter house. Brother Dan, over accessing his relationship with the Carter's and Annie, to his great disappointment was not invited.

Other than Annie there was only one other Sonny preferred the company of in Kendal Grove, Sassy. Since the first evening he stepped into her place she had nothing but pleasantries for him. It was not of a carnal nature, but nurturing. During her business hours or non business hours she made time for him and had a genuine interest in his affairs. "You picked a good girl," Sassy said after he told her about the events of his recent marriage. "She's young, she ain't dumb, and she ain't the cheating kind either. Take care of your family young man. Here's a little something for ya'll. It ain't much." "Miss. Sassy, you didn't have to do that," said Sonny. "I know I don't, like I said, I wanted too. Looka here, I know a man who is moving away to live with his daughter. His little house ain't much. It sits on five acres, way back off the road and most of it is overgrown. By-the-way, every married woman should have her own house." "A house Miss. Sassy, I don't know. That's a big step, isn't it?" "Come on son, let's do some figuring. The cost of the house is $450. You received some cash gifts didn't you? You received $25 from me; from the Carter's, $50; from Joe, $25; and from your people $50." He wondered how she knew each dollar amount of the cash gifts he received and he hadn't told her yet. "You told me you've already got $300 in savings that you're saving for a truck of your own, right? Take $100 from savings, add the $150 in gift money and you have $250. Now look at that the house is almost paid for. With the interest on the mortgage your note won't be more than $7 a month. As a helper you make $15 a week, right?"

Annie was so proud and grateful that Sonny, after two months of marriage and at the age of eighteen purchased, not rented, a four room house on the hill. It didn't have an indoor bathroom, so what, neither did her parents. It had electricity, a wood burning cook stove, a pump at the kitchen sink and an ice box. It also had a fireplace in the living area. Repairs to the property were minimal. The outhouse roof needed patching, a few loose floor boards here and there, and a few missing rungs in the tiny front porch railing needed replacing. Bertha was so excited about Annie's first house one would have thought it was hers. The minute she heard the news from Annie she began to pick out the fabric for the curtains, draperies, table cloths, bedspreads and furnishings. "Is it enough room for a kitchen or dining table?" Bertha asked. "What size bed will you have? Do you have closets or will you need a wardrobe? How large is the parlor? Oh, one big arm chair and a small sofa will fit, you say? We already have all of the baby furniture. Alright, alright we shall see what we can do." Up the hill to the forbidden land and around the bend Bertha drove with the six month pregnant Annie in the passenger seat. She arrived at Annie's new home with her full arsenal of cleaning supplies. Adorned in her least favored house dress, work shoes, apron, head scarf and her wash day sweater, she was determined to do battle against dust, dirt, grime and germs. She had ammonia, soap chips, baking soda, oil soap, bleach, mops, brooms, rags and buckets, and a hammer and nails. She was also determined to hang the curtains and draperies before the day was over. Annie handled the light cleaning and Bertha took on the heavy stuff. It was going to be a long day which didn't matter because lunch and dinner for the two had been prepared and was in the picnic basket awaiting hunger to strike.

The first Pott's grandchild was born in April of the following year in his grandparents shack. With the absence of Sonny away on long road trips it was a blessing Annie went into labor on a visit to her parent's home. Otherwise with the solitude of being the last house on the road, and no telephone, she would have given birth alone. Burrell, underfoot of the midwife, tried to provide every comfort possible for his discontented baby sister while awaiting the baby to come. It was only at the demand of his father he left her side. "Git out dare boy, dats woman work!" Thomas shouted. "Ain't no man eva been round dis close cept he brining de pap emself. I sa git out dat room boy!" Miles Jordon was a healthy seven and one-half pound boy. His birth was the cause for much celebration, and the party in Picker's Woods lasted for two days. Three more sons came after Miles. By the age of twenty, Annie had four boys.

Chapter Ten
ISAAC'S OBSERVATION

It had been six years since Lethea's passing. From what Isaac saw, as he watched with apathy his male customers entering the store who married a second time, a second marriage for him was completely out of the question. The second wives acted as if they had something or the other to prove. In addition, a lot of the second wives fooled around with their current husbands while they were married to their first wives. Besides, there was no need to think on it because there was no one in the world who could replace Lethea. There was no one who walked, talked, smelled or smiled like her. The only women who came close to her style were married to his best friends. For the first time in his entire life he actually envied another person. He envied his friends for their relationships with their wives. There will never be another for me, so I might as well accept it, he thought. He decided not to think about remarrying or women at all for that matter. He was convinced that all he needed to do was concentrate on being a good father to his little girl, and running his store.

Maintaining her long, thick hair was a chore. Lenora combed her hair and pulled it into a bun and fastened it at the nape of her neck. Afterward she put on her favorite gray dress with tiny pink flowers and slipped into her comfortable gray shoes to start her day. All four pairs of shoes were comfortable, she thought, as she went about straightening her closet. Cut out of different fabric, all of her dresses were patterned the same. Button up the front, bell sleeves, non form fitting and three inches below the knee. No matter what she liked her father would override her decision and pick and order the same style dress for his little girl. She didn't mind very much but at times she wanted to wear pretty dresses and higher heeled shoes like the other girls her age were wearing. She wasn't allowed to wear skirts, blouses or silk hose, and a girdle or high heels were strictly out of the question. At least wearing this type of shoe her feet never hurt, whether in black, brown, gray or white, she reasoned. Women at the store complained about their feet hurting and they wore high heels all of the time. To her their actions were a little foolish but who was she to cast blame. Breakfast was waiting for her as it was every morning on the dining room table. Besides Miss. Dottie being a good cook and a good housekeeper it was good to have someone who genuinely cared for both she and her father. She was overjoyed that her father persuaded (so he say's) Dottie to move in with them after her mother's death. Shortly after Lethea's funeral when the visitors, telegrams, cards and letters of regret stopped coming, Dottie intervened. "How is everything going with you and Lenora?" Dottie asked Isaac. "Alright," Isaac mumbled packing groceries in her cloth sack. "Are you doing the cooking, housekeeping and taking care of Lenora by yourself? Because I know Bertha is not up to helping much." "Uh ah," he mumbled. "Isaac, stop mumbling." "Yes," he replied. "Thank the Lord that child has good hair, because I don't know how in the world she would look walking around here. Looka yea Isaac, I want you to clean out Lethea sewing room off the kitchen. Send some of them youngsters over to my place that run in and out of here to pick up my things and move them over to your place. Today is Monday and that gives you six days to clean that room out before I move in on Monday next. I won't take no for an answer, and I'll see you at church on Sunday morning." No more was said between them until they greeted each other before the Sunday morning church service. In actuality it was a great relief to Lenora for Dottie to move in. She had spent countless rainy nights long before her mother's passing, wondering if Miss. Dottie's roof would give way and crush her.

Helping her daddy at the store was a part of her daily routine. Several changes had been made at the store with the exception of her grandfather's chair. The chair was still next to the pot belly stove, where he sat keeping her father's company during the store hours.

Many years had past since his passing but every so often she'd notice her father chuckle, smile, then look toward granddaddy's chair as if to acknowledge something said, or to share with him his thoughts. Only to see his expression change when he remembered his father was no longer there and the chair was empty. Life was a funny thing, she thought. Until that day she didn't comprehend the meaning of the expression "nothing stays the same." With as many changes she had endured during the past six years, the passing of her mother, her grandfather, her daddy's sulkiness, not to mention her growing up, the only thing that remained constant and steadfast other than the love of God was Chaz.

I love you Lenora were Chaz's parting words to her each day. In the evenings when she could get away they would meet in their secluded place, opposite the Hill, and above the town. There they felt that they were on top of the world. A clearing with a large rock to rest their backs sat next to a dog wood tree, where the smell of honeysuckle and jasmine loomed in the air, and purple, yellow and orange wild flowers bloomed. It was a beautiful place, their place to sit, talk and enjoy each other. The thought of their place helped the hours go by quickly while assisting her father and helping customers at the store.

Patricia and her girlfriends from the Hill, entering the store with their bantering and cackling, elevated the noise level to almost intolerable. They were paying customers, so they must be tolerated, thought Isaac. "How do I look in this dress, girl?" Patricia asked one of her girlfriends, eyeing herself in the full length mirror in the Ladies Corner of Howard's Grocery store. "Patricia that's the one," she said. "All the men will surely like this one." "What do you mean all of the men? I only have one in mind." Patricia turned again and viewed her reflection with delight. Her thoughts turned to Chaz, wondering how he would think she looked in the dress.

As a child she adored watching the older girls and ladies of Kendal Grove try on dresses and hats as they admired themselves in the mirror. It was her turn and she adored dressing up in front of an audience more than she thought she would. Whenever she went shopping it was an event to attend for all of the young ladies. She played the role of a runway model showing all the newest fashions available at the store. No one could wear, or show a dress like Patricia. She had the face, the figure and she looked good in whatever she wore. Grown men would pay her $5.00 to sit with them at Sassy's Place. This is like taking candy from a baby, she thought. The first time she was offered money to sit with a man at his table was unbelievable. She took to it, and learned to handle her business transactions discretely in order not to embarrass her gentlemen friends. In reality, discretion was an excuse for upping the cost for older men to $15 for the opportunity to sit with her. At the age of sixteen she made more money than most men she knew. Two hours at Sassy's on Tuesday night, two hours at Sassy's on Thursday night and five hours at Sassy's on Saturday night brought in enough money to keep her dressed in style. It was more money than her Granny made in six weeks taking in laundry. There ain't nothing wrong with sitting at an old man's table for an half hour or so and being nice. They don't touch me and I don't have to dance with them unless I really want to. Sitting there looking pretty and I get paid for it. Life is great, she thought. She was a real good looking girl at sixteen and she along with everyone else knew it. Every man young and old on the Hill wanted her including Ricky. Patricia wanted nothing to do with any of them. Her heart, soul and mind belonged to Chaz Carter. She only wished that she had saved herself for him and not have given way to curiosity.

Patricia called to Lenora and asked, "What, do you think of this dress?" "What, do you think?" Lenora replied to conceal her true thoughts. Every dress Patricia chose to buy was much too tight and too old for her age. "Why, on earth did I asked you? You wouldn't know, since you wear those mousey dresses and old lady shoes." Turning her attention back to her reflection in the mirror, Patricia said, "This dress really looks good on me, and I might buy it." The backhanded remark, hit Isaac like a large rock in the pit of his stomach. Lenora turned away, biting her lip to hold back tears, unfolding and folding the sweaters on display. Isaac wanted his customers to know that his daughter would look one hundred times better in that dress given any old day. Instead he asked, "Lenora, do you want to take a break." She assented without looking up from her task, and exited the store. How cruel the remark was. He wondered how long had this been going on. Dottie had mentioned that girl and her treatment of Lenora. The actual experience of it was something all together different.

Isaac could partly respond as Mrs. Casey, a former resident of Kendal Grove, inquired about Lenora's health and wellbeing. She had been speaking for some time and most likely explained why she was visiting on this particular day, but his mind was elsewhere. "She must be almost grown, thinking about graduating high school, courting and things like that? I know all three of my girls did at that age. I bet she's as pretty as her mother was. How old did you say she was, about fifteen or sixteen? Let me tell you, if that is the case, I bet you have to beat the suitors off with a stick." "Yes mam," was all he could say. He was thankful that Mrs. Casey was true to herself, a motor mouth. She was an elderly, sweet natured woman who could talk non-stop. On and on and on she went only stopping when Isaac said, "that will be $2.15. Can I get you anything else?" "No thank you, Mr. Howard." It was a pleasure seeing you again. Have a wonderful day," she said as she left the store. "Oh, my God," he said to himself. What have I done to our child Lethea? She is not nine years old anymore, she is sixteen. What have I done to her?"

Dinner was on the table and his napkin was in his lap. "Amen," Isaac said after grace. Before he put the first morsel of Dottie's succulent roast beef into his mouth, he had to ask his daughter a question. He turned to her at the dinner table and asked, "Lenora, are you happy?" "I love you daddy," she said. "Why, would you ask me that?" "I know you love me, daughter. Are you happy?" "I love Kendal Grove, Daddy." "Lenora that is not what I asked you. Be honest with me?" Lenora bowed her head and began to cry. "That's it!" was her father's reply. "I've already contacted your Grandmother Helen, and she is expecting you. I made my decision earlier today about this. You'll go to New York and finish your education." "Praise the Lord," said Dottie. "Miss. Dottie, daddy you don't want me here?" He put down his fork and spoke to his teenage daughter and not to his nine year old little girl for the first time. "Lenora, if it was up to me, I would remain selfish and you would stay here with me and never leave Kendal Grove. I never intended to be a selfish man, and I won't ruin your life by becoming more of one now. You could certainly stay here and remain the way you are, or you could go to New York and come back an accomplished woman. I am only explaining this to you because I love you, and I don't want you to think that you aren't loved and wanted. I can teach you many things and you can learn many things in Kendal Grove. Helen and Agnes can share with you things that I know nothing about. You'll be leaving for New York the day after tomorrow on the Noon train." Isaac's heart was breaking as he watched his daughter cry. "May I be excused," she asked. "Yes, you may," he answered. He had to excuse her immediately because it was only the pressure of his clenched fist against his clenched mouth which prevented him from crying out and running after his only child, his baby girl. There was no time for Lenora to do anything except cry and pack. She wouldn't be able to sleep, so she concentrated on what to tell Madeline, Ricky and Chaz the next day, especially Chaz.

It was February and the only talk of those in her class was about graduation in the Spring. Lenora never imagined that she would not graduate with her life long friends. Madeline was the first to notice Lenora's puffy eyes and runny nose on the cold winter morning. "What is it?" Madeline asked her best friend. Stopping her on the pathway to school they had taken together for what felt like forever. "What's wrong?" asked Chaz. Chaz and Ricky on the path a few steps behind them. Lenora choked on her words as rivers of tears flowed down her face. Chaz moving ahead of her could only think of one thing to do, turn around and embrace her. "What is it Lenora?" he asked. "I leave for New York, tomorrow at Noon." "Oh, my goodness!" said Madeline. "Did your Grandmother or Aunt pass away?" "No." "Then why are you leaving?" Ricky asked. "Because, because my father is sending me there to live." They were rendered incapable of speech. No words came to mind for them to deliver an adequate response. The only sound was Lenora's sobs, the rustling of the dry leaves blowing in the morning breeze, and the hawking of the crows overhead. "Please repeat what you said, again?" asked Chaz. "I'm leaving tomorrow to live in New York, and I'll be catching the Noon train. My father made the decision yesterday. My grandmother and Aunt are expecting me." Pulling herself together Lenora continued her walk to school. Bewildered, Madeline, Ricky and Chaz were left standing in the same place they stopped on the pathway. As if someone flicked a switch, in tandem, the three friends ran ahead to catch up with Lenora. "Just like that?!" Madeline asked. "Just like that," answered Lenora. "We'd better hurry, we're running late, and I have a note for the teacher."

Chapter Eleven
NEW YORK

Lenora had imagined her grandmother's home in New York many times. However, within the deepest depths of her mind she could not have imagined the lavishness of her three storied, stand stone Italianate home. There was a marble foyer, marble mantels in the parlors and bedrooms, and parquet floors throughout. It was elaborately furnished with hand woven floor coverings, thick and patterned portieres with brass hooks, some with fringe, and crystal chandeliers. There were two stained glass windows, one was oblong in shape over the front door and the other was a large Palladian window at the top of the first story stairs. On the first level, through the small vestibule and to the right of the foyer is the library and to the left is the formal parlor and beyond that is the dining room. Pass the dining room through the swinging door is the butler's pantry and behind the butler's pantry is an extensive kitchen. On the other side of the hallway is her Grandmother's parlor. Used for informal gatherings, writing letters and updating her itinerary. Next to her grandmother's parlor is the breakfast room. The three hired help were in the foyer to greet Lenora's arrival. Henry and Lizzy, the butler and maid, lived on the premises. The cook, Vessy, who made all of their meals, seven days a week, lived off the premises. An enclosed back porch off the kitchen was the Help's respite quarters. Two laboratories one for the use of family and guests and the other for the Help was also on the first level.

On the second story there were three bedrooms and two laboratories. Lenora grandmother's sitting room and bedroom was laid out in baby blue satin. An overstuffed davenport and two chairs in her sitting room surrounding the fireplace made a comfortable setting. In her bedroom, a king size mahogany, rococo poster bed, two mahogany nightstands, a mahogany dresser and chest of drawers to match were strategically placed to maximize space and comfort. Her dressing table was decorated in baby blue satin with white lace trim to match her bedspread. Flanked on either side of the dressing table were tall iron lamps designed to resemble candelabras. On the other side of her walk-in closet were French doors that led into her pink tiled laboratory. Complete with a walk-in shower, water closet and bathtub. Lenora's bedroom, located in the front of the house, was twice the size of her room in Kendal Grove, which gave her room for a sitting area. She too slept in a king size poster bed with a nightstand on either side. At the foot of her bed was a divan with the same floral pattern as her arm chair and foot stool. Her dressing table was done in beige satin with white lace trim to match her bedspread. Her desk matched her other furnishings, dresser and chest of drawers. The massive walk-in closet was adjacent to her laboratory. Lenora and Agnes shared a bathtub and shower, but had separate toilets and sinks. Agnes' room was also beautifully decorated and was located closest to the dumbwaiter, and the back stairs to keep her coming and goings, at all hours of the night, unnoticed by her mother. The stairs to the private quarters of the help on the third floor was accessed through a door at the top of the back stairs on the second floor.

Agnes was a successful artist, extremely social and seldom at home. She had a way about her that attracted men to her like calamari dangling on the end of a fisherman's line in overly stocked waters. A tall and slender, light brown skinned woman with long legs and long fingers that she gracefully played the piano with. Long silky black hair and doe eyed made her striking. Always on the make, her horned rimmed glasses gave the appearance of a naive bookworm. That was the bait to reel her quarry in. The instant a man who met her qualifications would engage in conversation with her, he was hooked, captivated by her looks, intellect and charm. Agnes had her own money left to her by her father in addition to a modest income she made selling her paintings. Talent never acknowledged by her mother or those of her mother's Circle. To get away from the prying eyes of the Circle, she and a few close knit pals spent four months out of the year at an artist colony in Mexico.

It took three tiresome weeks before Helen Franklin would deem her granddaughter appropriate for proper introductions to the Circle. The time had come for Lenora to meet her grandmother's dearest friend, Constance Beavin, the reigning queen of the Circle. Royce and Constance Beavin were the dream couple of the Harlem Circle. Royce, the handsome and successful founder and president of the Beavin Shoe Manufacturing Company was a calculating and shrewd business man. He viewed all competition as his enemy and showed no mercy to those involved with him in business matters. He was the epitome of "put up or I'll shut you down," which he did many times to previous competitors. Yet, when it came to his family he was the opposite. He was a loving, gentle and attentive father and totally devoted to his beautiful wife. Forward women who crossed his path making known their wicked desires to interfere with his marriage were driven from his presence embarrassed and in tears. Women found "grinning in his face", as he referred to it, would feel the brunt of his anger, and would have to listen to him spout the virtues of his wife. Constance was just as calculating and shrewd as her husband was in business, when it came to running her household and her social activities. She was a lady and was in total control of her family and their surroundings. However, to everything there was an exception. Instrumental in her daughter's marriage into the right family, the Aldors, she had no control over her son-in-law's early demise. Her daughter, Suzanne, was a widow at twenty-three, and Constance had no grandchildren.

Suzanne despised her father-in-law, Peter Aldor, but agreed to live at the Aldor's House to avoid moving back into her parent's home. Like her daughter, Constance didn't care much for Peter. Aldor House was a monstrosity, and she wanted her daughter at home with her, to keep a close eye on her. She only agreed to let Suzanne remain with the Aldor's to maintain a hold on any fiduciary claims on their fortune. How Suzanne could live in the same house with the Aldors was beyond her. The only thing that was attractive about the fat toad of a man and his possum faced wife, was their good family name and his even better family money. He came from a long line of cotton farmers. When emancipation for the slaves came about and forty acres and mule were offered, his people took as many acres and mules that they could get their hands on. Those that didn't farm cotton purposely purchased overgrown land. Overgrown land is undesirable to most. To the trained eye it's a goldmine. Timber, oak, cedar; seedlings, hemp for ropes, peed moss, etc. In turn they owned and operated saw mills and sold wood to furniture manufacturers. His family philosophy: "money is a product of land ownership." In other words, if you own land it should be making you money. And so they did. Her daughter got quite a bit of it, but it was time to find her another husband. Jacob Aldor would be a good pick for Suzanne. Their union would be to her liking, if he weren't opinionated, and he'd listen to her and do as he was told.

Lenora took one last look at her reflection as her grandmother brushed the imaginary lint from her shoulder. "Perfect," Helen said to Lenora. "Now, let's go down stairs. The car should be arriving any moment." Lenora was putting on her gloves as the door bell rang. Henry hurried to answer the door before it rang twice. "Yes, the ladies will be out in a moment," he said through the opened door. "Grandmother, I didn't know that taxi drivers wore black suits while driving," said Lenora. "As far as I know, they don't. We're being driven to the Beavins' in a private car, not a taxi. This is Sam," introducing Lenora to the driver. "Sam this is my granddaughter, Miss. Lenora Howard." Sam, slightly bent at the waist and tipping his hat, said, "Miss." "When I order a car, I request him." Sam held the back passenger door open of the sleek black Cadillac limousine, for the ladies. Closing the door, he returned to the driver's seat and waited for his instructions. "To the Beavins," said Helen. "Yes Mam," he replied. Helen continued, "There will be times when Miss. Lenora will need you to get her around town, Sam. I am sure I can depend on you for that." "Yes Mam, you sure can," said Sam. Lenora wondered why they were stopping first at an art gallery or museum as the car drove into the semi-circle driveway in front of a bleached limestone, three storied, corner building. At the sides of the federal style doorway, stone stairs lead to double oak doors with large brass door knockers, brass doorknobs and shinny brass kick plates. "We'll be ready for home at 3:00PM promptly," her grandmother told Sam as the front door opened. "Good afternoon, Mrs. Franklin," said Grayson the Beavin's Butler. "Good afternoon, Grayson. This is my granddaughter, Miss. Lenora Howard." "How do you do, Miss.," said Grayson. "May I take your coats?" "Fine, thank you. I believe Mrs. Beavin is expecting us?" "Yes, Mam, she will receive you in her sitting room." Grayson led them up the curved staircase to the sitting room, as if Helen had never been there before, and Lenora followed. Lenora could only sum up her thoughts regarding the house with one word, opulence! It was at the least 6,000 square feet of sheer grandeur. She noticed the mint green wallpaper, with green vines and humming birds sipping nectar from cardinal flowers, in the vestibule. Also in the vestibule were padded benches on either side covered in mint green fabric with dark green and yellow vertical stripes. At the other end, double doors with frosted windowpanes had the humming bird motif etched into the panes. The frosted windowed doors opened into a breathtaking, marbled rotunda foyer, she could not have envisioned in a private home. In the middle of the foyer was a large round cushioned, dark green, velvet settee, with a four foot statue of Aries stemming from it. Hug, high above it was the most beautiful crystal chandelier she had ever seen. Two fluted columns marked the entry to the spacious step down parlor to her left. She could see the plush seating area nearest the marble mantel fire place and the high gloss of the grand piano. To her right she concluded was the dining room, but closed pocket doors concealed her suspicions. As they ascended the staircase she could not help but to look around. She was amazed by the decorative window caps and wondered where on earth one could find the fabric and someone to make window coverings for 15' x 5' windows. Not fifteen inches by five inches, actually fifteen feet by five feet windows. My goodness, she thought. Lenora liked to make curtains and wondered how many windows were in the entire house and what size each window was. As they were announced, Lenora found that Constance's sitting room on the second floor was equally as beautiful.

The two old friends after exchanging kisses on each others cheek fell into comfortable report. Mrs. Beavin was very pretty and the resemblance to her Grandmother was uncanny. They looked like sisters and were approximately the same height, weight and light complexion. The only difference other than age was that Constance had green eyes and her Grandmother's eyes were brown. Lenora thought she had been forgotten until Constance said, "So this is your Granddaughter?" The young lady that sat before the queen of the Circle in a grey tailored suit was keenly summed up, (A-line skirt with a gray and white shirtwaist jacket to match, gray clutch purse, with matching shoes completed the ensemble, long, thick hair, bright eyes, dark with clear skin. Perfect posture with hands in her lap, legs closed at the knees and feet together, flat on the floor, simply lovely). "She is lovely, simply lovely," said Constance. "Lenora would you pour?" Constance asked to test her poise. She was pleased with Lenora's ease and grace as she served tea. From the country she may be and dark, very dark, yet she couldn't get over the child's aura that captivated her every thought. There was something special about this one, who had a smile and personality that could charm bees away from honey. She had to admit to herself that she was the most exquisite thing she had ever seen. It was time for a shake-up in the Circle and Lenora was right for it.

Home for the weekend and anxious to have some fun Kennis wondered how he could get passed his mother's open sitting room doors without being seen. "I know that's Helen Franklin's voice, but who does the other voice belong too?" He said to himself. "It's not Agnes. It's a young girl's voice." Oh no! He thought. "I hope it's not another dry and boring chip off the old Circle girl they're trying to set me up with again," he said murmuring. "No, not this time, I've got to make a run for it. If mother catches me, I'm sunk." "Kennis,

Kennis, is that you?" Constance called. Keep going, keep going old boy, he thought. "Yes mother," he answered. "Come in darling, there is someone I want you to meet." One look at Lenora and his hasty countenance was altered. Oh, my goodness, he thought, what have we got here? Kennis could no longer hear his mother speaking to him because he was engaged in his line of vision and his conversation with self. "Look at this black beauty," he said to himself. "Kennis, Kennis are you listening to me?" "Yes mother." "Please go on," he said accepting the tea cup and saucer handed to him by Lenora. "This is Lenora Howard, your Aunt Helen's granddaughter." Thank God she's not my real aunt, he thought. "Lenora has moved to New York to live with her Grandmother and will be attending the Everly School for Young Ladies. I hope you'll be hospitable to her, as she is new to our city." "I would be more than happy too, Mother." "Yes Siree, looks like this summer just became more exciting," he said to himself. But something was odd about this one. Her attentions were adverted elsewhere, and she never looked his way without purpose. This was unusual for a girl, especially a dark one. He drank his tea first standing up than sitting down. He walked over to the window, in front of her, and peered out at invisible objects, than sat down again. Then he displayed his most debonair and handsome fellow routine, ambling to and fro around the room. Not one glance did she make in his direction. He knew because he couldn't keep his eyes off of her. How could he not look at her beautiful face? He tried to resist it but it was to no avail. "Kennis, don't you hear me speaking to you, are you still here?" "Yes, Mother." "Since you are right here, let's make it official." "What's that mother?" "Oh, Kennis, where is your mind? We're talking about the Jones' this Saturday and the Barkley's a week from Saturday. We thought that is Helen and I, thought it would be a wonderful idea for you to escort Lenora to both events." If he could display on the outside what he felt on the inside, he was sure they would lock him up in an insane asylum. Yet, he responded with a humble, "Yes Mother, I'd be happy too." Lenora looked in his direction for the second time. The first time she looked in his direction was when they were introduced. She gave a faint hint of a smile when the two great friends agreed on an appropriate time for Kennis to pick up Lenora for their first evening out together. "Oh, Kennis, darling, do you think she should meet Shelton and Milo before the others?" Not on your life Mother this one is mine he wanted to reply. Instead he said, "No Mother, I think she can meet them when she meets the others."

Kennis, Milo and Shelton were born into the Circle and did almost everything together. Buddy's long before entering the private and exclusive Academy for Young Men. Attending the same college together was no exception. They lacked talent, creativity and chief characteristics such as chivalry, kindness or consideration. And their devil-may-care attitude was accepted and hailed as a trait of the privileged. Their clout, money and good looks took them wherever they wanted to go. Kennis, the Zachary Scott look-a-like with fuller cheeks and lips, was the most handsome. He was "tantalizing," as one girl put it visiting the campus for the Spring Dance. The same girl, who after making an outright play for Kennis, wound up behind the shrubbery of the Hall where the dance was held dry humping Shelton after drinking the four cups of punch laced with moonshine he had given her. Shelton who stood a half inch under Kennis liked shunned woman or crybabies as he put it. "Pat them up, make them feel better, and they'll give it up in a second!" Shelton said. "Tell them how wonderful they are, and what a fool "he" was to let them slip away. After the deed is done they always ask, "Shelton, does this mean we are a couple?" My response in my most humble repose: "Me you want me? Oh darling, I was lucky to spend time with you. The truth is you are too good for me and you deserve someone better than me. We will always remain friends and what happened between us will forever be between me and you. Whenever you need me girl, you call me and I'll be there for you." That's the best line fellows, because they keep on calling and I keep getting all the loving I want with no strings." It was in college where the pudgy Milo, who stood the same height as Shelton, confirmed his bachelorhood. It was the

Assistant Chancellor's wife who helped him come to that conclusion. "Why get married and have to deal with responsibility, when I can get all the loving I want from lonely wives," he said. Spend a few dollars here, a few more there and let them cry on your shoulder a little bit. Wipe their tears, give them what they want, get what I want and send them back to their husbands." When it came to woman they were dregs. They knew it and relished in it.

Lenora had been in New York for three weeks and hadn't been to church since she left home. The enormous stone edifice with cherubim's carved around the bell tower of the African Methodist Episcopal Zion Church was nothing like the little one room sanctuary with the fellowship hall attached in Kendal Grove. It was the size of a half block with four entrances into the main sanctuary. Stairs on either side of the entrance hall leading to a balcony and at least one hundred pews in which to choose divided into three sections on the main level. The inside resembled the great cathedrals in a tourist brochure of Rome with its elongated picturesque stained glass windows, carvings, tapestries and golden sacred instruments. Lenora had no idea where to sit. Her Grandmother led her to the front of the church to the center row of pews where the family names of the most prominent parishioners were engraved. The first pew in the front was simply engraved Pastor; the second pew Aldor; the third pew Everly the fourth pew Beavins, the fifth pew was engraved Hollis and the sixth was engraved Franklin. The sixth pew from the pulpit in the center isle was only used by the Franklin family and their guests. It was there Lenora, her Grandmother and Aunt Agnes sat to worship.

The waiting list to attend the Everly School for Young Ladies was more than three years long. An Everly graduate, held in the highest esteem, was expected to be articulate, learned and cultured. The curriculum included: English, English Literature, Foreign Language (French), Social Studies, Negro Studies, Science, Biology, Chemistry, Math, Algebra, Trigonometry, Art, Music, Home Sciences and Elocution. The tedious application process for Lenora was waived and she was immediately accepted to join the senior class. Her

Grandmother being best friends to both its founder, Madame Vasti Everly, and her sister, Mrs. Constance Beavin was to her favor. In total there were no more than thirty-six girls in attendance at a time. There were twelve at the primary level, twelve at the junior and twelve at the senior level. With Lenora in attendance there would be thirteen graduates. Her apparel to attend the prestigious Everly School had been selected and fitted as well as her apparel for the many day and evening events she would attend weekly. The façade of Everly was similar to that of her Grandmother's house. Exteriorly the difference was defined by the stone entryway with columns, interiorly there were no similarities. Girls of all ages were chatting and mingling in the salon before classes began when Lenora entered the school on her first day. The Head Mistress rang the handheld bell and the girls dispersed to their prospective classes. The spacious salon on the entry level doubled as an all purpose area for receptions, play productions and graduation ceremonies. The dining room, kitchen and offices, occupied by the Founder and the Head Mistress were also on the same level. The entirety of the second floor, except for the teacher's lounge and the powder room, was designated for teaching primary and junior curriculum. The third floor was where Lenora and her senior classmates were taught. A bright student and easy to make friends, Lenora excelled in all of her classes at Everly and made many friends. Her girlfriends, attractive in their own right, and very much apart of the Circle, had varied personalities that complimented the others. Barbara Naylor, considerate and understanding, always looked forward to the next fun and exciting project to complete. Cheryl Glad, knowledgeable and always thinking of those closest to her, knew the right thing to say in every situation. Rita Hatchfair, posed a rough attitude, which starkly contradicted her tenderheartedness and her infectious laugh. Dee Hockling and Carmen Frank, verbose, possessed hearts of gold. Tracy Washington, kind and tenderhearted, had the ability to turn a tragedy into a comedy. Robertlene Tenstall had an opinion about everything whether warranted or not. Pamela Miller, the observer, sat back and watched everyone play out their lives before her, expounding her wisdom when coaxed or agitated.

"Do you like attending the Everly School for Young Ladies?" Kennis asked during his Easter break from college. "It's wonderful," answered Lenora. Everly was a vast difference from the four room schoolhouse she attended in Kendal Grove, but she didn't mention it. It wasn't because she was ashamed of the two and four room schoolhouses that dotted the landscape of Crystal County, somehow she knew Kennis could not relate. "Madame Everly is so elegant, and is held in the highest regard," said Lenora. "She has green eyes like your mother." "Yes, she does. They get the color of their eyes from their father whom they never speak of. Aunt Vasti's husband, my Uncle Ev was held in high regard also. Let me tell you a little bit about her husband. The late Iverson Benton Everly, III who owned four barber shops, and promoted small purse fights. His hands were into a little of everything. There were two shops down south, where he was from, which were run by his cousin and two shops in Harlem. It was the goings-on in the back of the Harlem barber shops, and the prize fights that made him a wealthy man. His connections were with those in the city who could make things happen good or bad depending on which side you stood. That kept him both in the know and in the doe," Kennis said. "Yet, it didn't keep him from being killed by one of his disgruntled customers. This particular customer after more than thirty years of service retired and decided to take his entire pension check to the barber shop instead of to the bank. It was a lot of money to him but he knew he couldn't live off of it for the rest of his life. He thought he could double it or maybe triple it at Ev's place. To make a long story short Ev cashed the check, charged him a fee, and then took all of his money in under a half hour in a game of craps. The customer fell to his knees and begged Ev for his money back. Of course it was no go with Ev. The man got up from his knees and pulled a knife from his boot. When he was refused again he stabbed Ev in the throat. That day both Ev and the customer lost their lives because Ev's body guards killed the customer straight away. You do know that Uncle Ev and your Grandfather were partners? The market may have crashed but our families weren't solvent. Did you ever think of that? Your Grandfather was the one who handled all the figures." "Figures, he handled what figures?" "Yes, numbers, money." "No, I didn't know that." "Uncle Ev had to leave New York in and hurry, if you get my drift? He hid out as a picker in the tobacco fields of Maryland, where he met your Grandfather. Whatever those two put together by "hook or crook", as the old folks used to say, worked and the money piled in. When Uncle Ev was given the "o.k." to come back to New York your Grandfather, Grandmother and Aunt came back with him. They owned an insurance business, but after the death of your Grandfather, Uncle Ev didn't have much interest in running it, and the business was sold for a good profit. You really didn't know they were partners, my Uncle Ev and your Grandfather?" "No, I didn't," answered Lenora. Some of the stories that Kennis told Lenora were very far reaching. Lenora could never tell if the stories were true or not. Over time she learned that the majority of what Kennis told her was true. It was through Kennis' eagerness to spill every juicy detail of her family's secreted life she came to understand Agnes' odd behavior. "She is very much into the free thinking and the free love movement," he said. "The institution of marriage was an overrated and outdated concept to her. The idea of commitment and being with one sexual partner for the whole of ones life was like being in prison. She has had many lovers, although, none married. Her men differ in age, size and race." So that is why Agnes snapped at me, "Mind your business!" Lenora thought. All I did was ask her why she was leaving the best party of the season so early in the evening. In other words, as Kennis summed it up, she had other fish to fry and her kind of fish couldn't be found in that crowd. That is unless someone new came along for her to seduce.

New York had so many different types of people. There many types of people that spoke different languages, French, Italian, Polish, Russian, German, Chinese and the Jewish people that spoke Yiddish. There were Japanese people but most were in internment camps while the war was going on. There were people who looked Negro but did not identify themselves with the Negro's of America. She met dark skinned people from Africa, Jamaica, Panama, Ethiopia, Costa Rica, Cuba and Brazil. New York was a big and wonderful place to live and explore with its sky scrapers, the Statue of Liberty, the Empire State Building, ferries and the subway system. She had actually ridden the "A Train." She truly enjoyed living in Harlem with its apartment buildings, brown stones, cathedrals, schools, restaurants, theaters, night clubs and famous ballrooms. At home the county fair was a must to attend to mark the end of the summer but it couldn't compare with Coney Island and its beach.

Lenora wondered how the Chadwell sisters would take Greenwich Village. There anyone could do anything they wanted and considered it a free expression of art? White men were with Negro women and white women with Negro men. Men danced with men and women danced with other women, and gave the impression that they were madly in love with one another. Her first visit to Greenwich Village was how the French say a? sensation! Escorted by Kennis Beavin of Beavin and his close circle of friends to see the Free Impressionist of Our Time art exhibit was one unforgettable day. No warning ever came from Kennis, Milo or Shelton on what to guess would come next. She found herself in a world of astonishment, just on the sane side of sheer mania. Neither he nor his friends were moved the slightest bit by the unusual sites. "Keep your composure, and don't stare whatever you do," she repeated to herself over and over again until finally they arrived at the intended venue. Greeted and ushered into the art exhibit by an overly dressed, tall, slinky blonde woman with big hands and an Adam's apple, Lenora found it difficult to believe that she found the artwork breathtaking. There wasn't a piece she didn't instantly fall in love with and wanted to purchase. She had heard that real artists were a bit peculiar, which she experienced by her Aunts behavior, but this was nothing like anything peculiar she had experienced before. The art, the artist and Greenwich Village was an unusual place but the people who lived and frequented there were nice and seemed happy. She giggled to herself because the question wasn't what would the Chadwell Sisters think of Greenwich Village but what would Greenwich Village think of the Chadwell Sisters?

Yes, New York was a place to behold but she missed her father, and the quite rural landscape of Kendal Grove. She would remain in New York attend Teachers College and receive her certificate. Uncertain if she would stay on in New York to teach or go home and teach. Lately no matter what she found herself doing either alone or not her mind would drift home to Kendal Grove. Although, sometime difficult she could smell spring in the air amidst the varied aromas of carbon monoxide, food, perfumes and street dust. She remembered that this time of year was her mother's favorite. The air smelled so fresh and sweet and the trees and flowers were beginning to blossom. Mother birds, robins, finches and sparrows littered the lawns of Kendal Grove forging for insects and worms and the black birds filled the trees. Occasionally, the striking colors of the blue jay or a cardinal or a humming bird sipping nectar could be spotted. Or sighting a red plumed woodpecker and hearing the unmistakable reverberation of its beak hammering away at the speed of lightening on trunk of a tree. Or seeing a white tailed deer or the smell of lilac or later during the summertime when the moon and the fireflies lit up the night. What she didn't miss was the sighting of a green garden snake slithering through the garden foliage or worse a lengthy black snake slithering across the yard or across her path on a dusty dirt road.

She learned from Madeline's faithful letters that Annie had a baby boy. Five months later there was news of a passing, a wedding, and someone else awaiting a blessed event. The mail was delivered two hours late when the next letter arrived from Madeline. The contents of the letter made Lenora wish it had never come. She was unprepared for the news and almost fainted when she read the last line of the letter: "Chaz and Patricia have married and are expecting a child." Her sudden gasp broke the tranquility of the evening in her Grandmother's parlor listening to their favorite weekly radio broadcast. "What is it child?" asked Agnes putting her arms around Lenora to steady her. "Oh, my goodness," her Grandmother said after picking up the letter and reading the last line. Lenora bolted for the telephone as her Aunt too read the telling words of her niece's alarm. Lenora hadn't made a long distance telephone call before not even to her father but with this news, she must. She forewent asking her grandmother's permission to place the long distance call. "Hello, long distance," she said with urgency. "I want to make a person to person call to Madeline Trusdale of Kendal Grove, Maryland. Yes, I'll hold."

"Kennis," called Constance. "Yes mother," he answered. "You are, Lenora's escort for this year's Cotillion, yes?" "Yes mother, of course I am. That is if you haven't already promised me out to someone else, again." "No, not this year son, your job is escorting, Lenora. And son, I would like to add that you are doing a splendid job with her. I couldn't be more pleased to see you with anyone else as when I see you with her." Usually, Kennis would be found in a parlor chair sunken into a disparaged sitting position, unwillingly agreeing to every word his mother said to keep the peace. When mother is happy the entire house is happy. That was his father's motto as well as his, his sister's and their servants. But this conversation interested him. Why, because for the first time ever he would be escorting someone that he wanted to be with. In addition, she was the prettiest girl coming out into society. And as far as everyone was concerned except Lenora, she was his girl.

His widowed sister sat silently listening to her mother's connotation. Her voice danced when she spoke of Lenora. The tone was familiar because it was the same when she spoke of her marriage to Reginald Aldor. The Aldors and their cotton farms, land and lumber mills were the only family that could surpass the Beavins. Financially that is. By all other accounts class, style and looks the Beavins had them beat. Suzanne Beavin Aldor married, widowed and childless at the age of twenty-three. She had been very fond of her late husband of two years. They were very good friends before they married and despite the circumstances remained so while he lived. She should have hated him but she couldn't, no one could hate Reginald. What their parents didn't know was that Reginald was a closet alcoholic and enjoyed sex with both men and woman, preferably men. She was sick and tired of hearing "you are too young to be a widow and no children," and then they would shake their head and walk away. She wanted to scream no we didn't have any children because we seldom had sex, because he preferred men over me. But she held her silence and would take his secrete to her grave. She didn't keep much of anything from her brother and could scantly keep her mother from finding out anything. She wondered if Kennis knew about his brother-in-laws sexual anomaly and didn't tell her for fear of their mother's wrath if they didn't marry. Kennis, like his Mother, knew almost everything about everybody, and if he wasn't told personally, he would find someway to get it out of you. It was Kennis who tricked her into telling him that she wasn't a virgin the day she married. It was all Reginald's fault he used to be so much fun and at one time he could talk her into anything. "Come on Suzanne have another drink, come on Suzanne let me touch you there," he'd say. "Come on Suzanne let me look at it. Come on Suzanne what difference would it make, it's me baby and we're getting married in a few days." What she experienced with him that night was great. If that was sex she wanted a lot more of it. What she didn't presume was after the honeymoon sex between she and her husband would be rare. Most of her nights were spent alone without her husband and during the day he worked tirelessly at his office. Family events were the only time available to her to spend with her husband. If by chance he came home and wasn't too inebriated the possibility to indulge in passionless sex might arise. It was more times than thought possible she went without the basic function of a married couple. Any judge would grant an immediate divorce based on that alone but that would mean scandal and Constance Beavin would not stand for that. Despite Reginald being a closet alcoholic and homosexual she loved her dear departed husband, but mourning him was for the birds. She was young attractive and needed and wanted her passion returned.

After the death of Reginald his parents insisted Suzanne sublet their apartment and move in with them. She was convinced that their urgency was in the hopes that she could be carrying their son's child and didn't want another man to get involved with her and take credit. Thanks to Reginald's one night of too much alcohol on a rainy night her freedom from her mother's uncompromising eyes had been curtailed. Her days consisted of breakfast at home with the Aldors and lunch and dinner with her family at their home. "Hey, sis," Kennis said greeting his sister before dinner. "Hey is for horses, Kennis." "My dear sister, Suzanne," he said standing and bowing to her. "You'll never guess who, I saw today?" "No, I wouldn't," she said, pretending not to be interested. "Jacob Aldor, the cousin of Reginald's. He's opening another movie house at the end of next week. Do you want to go?" "I'll let you know," she replied. She didn't want either of them to notice her excitement at the mention of his name. "Who did you take tea with this afternoon, darling?" Constance asked Suzanne. "The regulars mother, Thelma, Eunice and Katherine." "Is there anything new to speak of?" "No, nothing new, this week, Mother." Suzanne lied because there was continuously something new going on with her closest girlfriends. From experience she knew not to share a word of it with her mother, as it would be the topic at the next Women's Club meeting. Nor did she want her mother to know that after tea she met, Jacob Aldor. He always had a soft spot for Suzanne and the loss of his cousin brought them closer. They had become romantically involved over the last several months and Jacob was more than ready to ask Suzanne to marry him. His only hesitation was that he despised her mother. Constance Beavin was every bit of a lady in the eyes of her husband and the Circle but in reality she was a controlling, manipulative and spiteful woman. He did not want her involved in their lives. How could he marry Suzanne and keep Constance out of their lives? They would have to move, but where? He would have to brainstorm and come up with an idea to keep Constance far away from them and completely out their lives.

The time flew by in New York. Lenora had graduated the Everly School for Young Ladies and was in her final year of Teachers College. Her calendar remained full she and her school chums stayed on the move. If it wasn't a school or church activity, it was a social or charitable event to attend. On another visit to Greenwich Village for a sold out concert, Kennis told Lenora that his parents were extremely fond of her. "If I were to ask you to marry me it would be a win situation," said Kennis. "Why do you say that Kennis?" "My parents would be happy. I am sure your Grandmother would be happy, and you would be lucky to have me." "What did you say, Kennis Beavin?" asked Cheryl. Before he could respond Robertlene chimed in with, "You mean it would be the other way around." "I didn't ask for any comments from the troop." "Gee wiz, Kennis, you've got to be the most arrogant guy I know," said Pamela. "Ladies, ladies you know the routine," said Tracey. "Ignore him, and let's go inside." Kennis gently pulled Lenora aside before entering the venue with the others. "Lenora did you hear what I said?" he asked. "Kennis Beavin you are a pain." "Lenora, why would you say a thing like that? Out of the four years you've been in New York we've been going out steadily for three of those years. I am a great catch." His ego brought her so much amusement. "Kennis," Lenora said, as she faced him with her delicate candor and beautiful smile. "I am sure that is what all of the other young ladies you take out tell you. Please explain to me why you think you are such a good catch." "It's not because some of the girls tell me that but it goes without saying, I am heir to successful shoe business. My father is not just in the business of selling shoes, he also manufacturers shoes. You know that's highly unusual for a Negro, and he has contracts all over the country. I am light skinned with good hair, very handsome, well-groomed and educated. I have less than one year of college left, and we could be married in August right after my graduation. We could live with my parents." "So, you have it all planned out for me. What about me teaching?" "You wouldn't work. My Mother would love to have you as company during the day in that big old twenty-nine room house. Lenora you could continue your social work with poor children, your church activities and you could teach Sunday school. You and my Mother love to do the same things, you could have tea parties and social fund raisers all the day long." "Kennis, I am in New York to continue my education, but my heart is in Maryland. Suppose I decide to go back home to teach after I finish school? Believe me Kennis, I cannot imagine you in my home town where the men go fishing and hunting. For some reason, I don't think the outdoorsy life suits your taste." "Who is talking about living in your hometown with the exception of you? If you do make the decision to go back to Kendal Grove, change it. Women do it all of the time. There is no other way to look at it. Lenora, you have to marry me because I don't know anyone else my family cares for as much as they do you." "What about love and romance, Kennis?" "Lenora, what are you talking about? I practically take you everywhere I go during my summer vacation and when I am home on break. You're the only one I let come up to visit me on special occasions at school. On all accounts you are my girl. You're the one on my arm, the one that is allowed in my home during family events. I do love you, and I want you to be my wife. What is wrong with that?" Taking a deep breath and shaking her head from side-to-side, she chose her words carefully before speaking. For fear of losing her composure and telling him what she really felt which would crush his ego, and ruin their friendship. "Kennis, let's discuss this later," she said before entering the theater.

Lenora was different alright. She had both beauty and brains. She is dark, lovely and wonderful, he thought. She passed all of my tests. She knows the works of and can recite Shakespeare, the works of Thoreau, Elliott, Lawrence and Keating. When I asked how she knew her way around a library, she told me she founded the Kendal Grove Library.

Lenora's privilege to visit the library at the campus where her godfather had become the Dean of Philosophy gave birth to the idea that Kendal Grove needed a library too. She'd never been to a college campus and was impressed by the nine building rectangular shaped campus. There were two dormitories, one for males and the other for females. The instructors quarters, a science and math building, an English and humanities building, a gymnasium, cafeteria and auditorium. There also was an agricultural and carpenters workshop building adjacent to five acres of farmland and an administrative building. Most impressive to Lenora was that the space at the top of the administration building housed the campus library. It was an expansive two story area that measured fifteen hundred square feet. A beautiful carved half mooned shaped counter was centered approximately fifteen feet from the libraries entrance. The curved staircases to the left and to the right of the entry led to the second floor. The catalog and card files were positioned a short distance behind the libraries counter and the walls were lined with five shelved cherry bookcases filled with books. Chairs and tables were neatly and strategically placed throughout the space to provide the ideal setting for study. The eight Palladian windows, three on both sides of the room, one in the front and another in the back provided more than ample light on the first floor. Three oil burning lamps with green shades were placed in the center of each table to provide light for evening study. And two large pot belly stoves, one at the front of the room and one at the back, mounted on brick harts with long stove pipes to carry the smoke and embers away from the books were there to keep the students warm in the winter. She observed that the same layout also applied to the second floor of the library with the exception of the card files.

Lenora was so impressed by the college campus, its faculty, students and the library that all the way back home she contemplated ways to begin a library in Kendal Grove. Her father donated an acre of land on which sat a small dilapidated house that was no longer inhabited and the potential library patrons jumped in to do the rest. Stones, bricks, lumber and other building materials were gathered and donated by Kendal Grove's residents. A few people who lived on the Hill and some of the pickers also donated what they could from their meager earnings. The original twenty by twenty-five feet structure was gutted, given a twin structure, built out and the Kendal Grove library was constructed. No money to buy books, Lenora began a letter writing campaign for donations. Her thirty-five letters accumulated donated books from Negro churches, schools and colleges to fill the shelves. Opening day was a proud day for Kendal Grove. There was a private reception for the library patrons and then it was time to open the doors to all. It was a year in the making but it was a great day for Kendal Grove.

Damn! Kennis thought. She is definitely marriage material for me, the one to take home to meet mother. But I don't have to take her home to meet my mother, because she already knows my mother and my mother, remarkably, has a true fondness for her. "Kennis, old boy," he asked himself, "What the heck is going on here?" You are thinking of spending quite time, your life with a woman and not just thinking of balling her brains out on any given day. You're talking about a good girl and your mother being fond of her. Oh man, you hate her friend, Ricky Stone, who she writes too, and is far away in the military, because they grew up together. You hate that guy Chaz, the one she never speaks of but know she is thinking of. He is in a place, a deep place within her, the place where I should be. Chaz, what kind of name is that? The country punk. I've got to snap out of this thought pattern. I'm calling someone a name I don't know? Am I in love? I must pay Dalcy a visit real soon so that I can be reminded that I'm not the falling in love type of guy. I am Mr. Kennis Bandeaux Beavin. How did Circular Magazine put it: "Mr. Kennis Bandeaux Beavin, the young, handsome and debonair son of Harlem's Shoe Mogul." Let me change the subject. Dalcy, Dalcy, think about the first time she let you touch her. What words would you use describe that particular moment? Passion or lust or the two intertwined? Kissing with our mouths open and tongues touching, she taught me how to do that on the first date. The way her covered breast felt in my hands. And then when disrobed there were two large light toasted brown buns with two dark brown dime size extensions calling me closer, and I sucked on her nipples like a small child who had not been weaned from its mother. Her nipples surrounded by silver dollar size brown areolas were the right size for my mouth. He smiled as he remembered thinking he was about to die because his heart was pounding so fast at the thought of reaching out to touch her breast. It was the real thing and not the pictures of natives in foreign places found in the explorer's magazines. From then on he knew he had to have that fast talking, gum smacking, hips swinging Sparks' girl. Thinking of her could bring his male senses to its peak, notwithstanding looking at her causing it more. Yet, Dalcy was not the type to ever take home to his mother.

Lenora wasn't privileged to the notion that Constance had once had her eyes set on Gretchen Hollis for her son. She was quite attractive, wealthy and knew and acted like she was considered the greatest match for every young man in the social circle. That was until, Lenora, his "Black Pearl," as the Circle referred to her, came onto the scene. Gretchen was as equally arrogant as she was boring. It was after the most humdrum date with Gretchen, his cousin Quinton, and his boring future wife Blanch, he met Dalcy for the first time. "Where are we off to Quinton, home?" he asked after safely depositing the boring Blanch and Gretchen at their prospective homes. "Home, after what we went through with Blanch and Gretchen," Quinton answered. "No, my boy it's off to life. I've got to park my car and pick up another from a mechanic friend of mine, and we are going to Sparks." "The Sparks, what on earth could be there for us?" Kennis asked with a disgruntled look on his face. "Life my dear boy life," Quinton replied. This is life? Kennis thought as they passed one dark, dingy and dank street after another. Garbage, mangy cats, dogs and people were indiscriminately dispersed on the streets of Sparks. It was late, very late on a Saturday night and loud talk and loud music permeated his ears. Doors slamming and people cussing, fussing and fighting all hours of the day and night was normal in Sparks. The place was unreal to the shoe manufacturing heir. "Why is this dingy place called, Sparks?" Kennis asked. "The combination of coal dust and ash that comes from the train tracks, and the dirty smoke that comes out of the factory chimney's can make it look like early evening on a bright, clear sunny day. You can imagine what it looks like on a cloudy day when you can faintly see to get around. With that in mind the one thing you can continually see are the sparks from the train wheels on the track. Hence the name, Sparks." Kennis asked again, "Why are we going to the Sparks?" "The Sparks is where you go to shake off what we just went through. Yes, Blanch is my girl and my intended, but I'm going to a look-a-like of what I really want." "What?" Kennis replied as he did not have a clue to what his cousin was talking about. "The family says that I have to marry, Blanch. Her skin is the right shade, her family has money and she is a part of the Circle. In reality, I don't want Blanch. I like curvaceous brown skin woman with beautiful smiles, quick to laugh and who like to dance. Do you know who the girl of my dreams was? Carrie Hamton. Remember her from summer school? She has no money, and the family considers her too dark." "Yes, I remember Carrie. She's a sweet girl, and one of the most pretty." "Not enough though for our family." "Isn't Gretchen dark, compared to us?" "Actually, she's about the color of peanut brittle." "Is that dark?" "No it isn't. She's acceptable because she can pass the paper bag test. Get it? Carrie couldn't. By-the-way, my name in Sparks is Charles Butler and tonight your name is Ken. Don't forget your name is Ken Butler. Oh yea, and if you like this cousin and you want to go back for more, you'll need to buy a jalopy, and rent a garage to keep it in with some extra clothes. You don't want to wear your good clothes or drive your nice car to Sparks. Unless that is you don't care about your station in life. Let me know what you decide after we leave tonight. If you need me too, I'll help you set everything up." Quinton was on his way to see his Rosa and on this particular night Rosa was having her cousin Dalcy spend the night.

Yes, Dalcy was what his mother referred to as a whole lot of yellow gone to waste, yellow trash. But she was some good feeling trash. She was hands on her hips, chewing gum popping, bows on her shoe, bright red lipstick and red nail polish wearing, yellow hussy trash. Oh yes, Mrs. Constance Beavin would faint straight away, if she got one look at Miss. Dalcy Bash and me walking arm in arm down any street. What would their conversation be like? "It's very nice meeting you

Dalcy," Mother would say. Dalcy would answer, "uh ha." "What does your father do for a living?" "He's in charge of slopping the hogs at Henderson's Pork Yard in Sparks. He's been there for years. You should hear my momma giving him the what for when he comes in at night. After all of these years he will still try to wear his slop boots across her kitchen floor." Then Dalcy would rare back and let go with her gigantic laugh while slapping her knee. Mother would be a gasp! I know that would put her under for sure. No, Miss. Dalcy is fine where she is and that is far, far away from my mother.

Dalcy was captivated by Kennis or Ken as she knew him to be. Her Prince Ken was the most thoughtful and caring young man she knew. He brought her and her mother lovely gifts, big and small, candy, jewelry, flowers and shoes. And than there were the large gifts like the new sofa, arm chair, desk, side chair, side tables, lamps, wall hangings, draperies, a rug, a kitchen table with four matching chairs; and a heardboard and mattresses for Dalcy's bedroom. Dalcy and her mother were proud recipients of his gifts that were previously slated for the dump. Constance had decided it was time to refurnish the quarters of the help and ordered new furnishings. When the new furniture arrived the old furniture was loaded on a truck for removal. Kennis intercepted the truck at a safe distance from his home and rerouted it to the Bash's. Dalcy's mother may have been impressed by the handsome young gift giver but her father didn't care much for him. Walter Bash knew that Ken was shady, but he couldn't identify it. He didn't want to accept gifts from Ken but he couldn't bring himself to deny his wife and daughter pleasantries he couldn't provide with his pay of $8.00 a week. At the pork yard he was a big man, the first Negro line supervisor. With his salary from the pork yard and the money from his side jobs he was able to purchase the four unit apartment building they lived in. Compared to others living in Sparks they were at the top of the echelon. They made it through tough times and through the depression without counting on the Sparks Mission for handouts like so many others did.

The pretty new furniture made the deteriorating condition of the interior of the apartment obvious. Dim lighting and veiled lamp shades could no longer conceal the pure ugliness of it all. The dirty and worn living room rug, moth eaten curtains, rotting kitchen floor, crumbling plaster and peeling paint throughout could no longer be overlooked. Kennis unwittingly had become a catalyst for Walter to put to use his side job skills to improve his own property both inside and out. The Landlord spent his evenings and Sunday afternoons, after church services, tackling the landscaping by trimming the trees, shrubbery and high grass and clearing debris including the overflowing trash bins at the front of and behind each unit. He then repaired loose railings, broken steps, porch floor boards, shutters and window panes. After priming the two-story wooden structure he painted it kelly green and reattached the newly painted white shutters before turning his interest to the undertakings inside. With the same gusto broken plaster was replaced, walls were painted, wooden floors refinished, kitchen and bathroom floors retiled, cabinets repaired and door knobs, door hinges and door handles tightened. It took months but his home looked like a showplace. The intensive labor was worth it, because for the first time in his life he had an aesthetically pleasing place to call home.

The thing that bothered him most about Ken was that he and Dalcy didn't go anywhere outside of their home. As far as he knew they had never officially been on a date of any kind. He dropped by on bowling night or lodge meeting night or the night of some other event. Those were the evenings when he and Dalcy would be left home alone. It's a shame she doesn't go for that Leroy Jones, he thought. She hasn't looked at him twice since Ken started seeing her. He's a nice boy and is starting to make a name for himself at the pork yard. He would love to take my baby out and proudly show her off on his arm everywhere he went.

Kennis' intentions excluded taking Dalcy anywhere except to her bedroom. He only had one thing in mind for his evenings in Sparks and didn't want to take a chance at being seen with her. Other men of his class were doing the same as he in Sparks and practiced discretion. It was no blemish on ones social reputation to take part in such activities, unless caught, and it was made known to the Circle. He had his methods of persuasion down to a science and put them into practice each time her parents left and turned the corner at the end of the block. He hoisted her sweater and bra under her neck before he turned her around and bent her over the kitchen table. One of her legs was fully extended to the floor and the other was bent at the knee propped on the kitchen table he bought them. She wasn't wearing any panties as was the custom when he came for a visit. Her stockings were held firmly in place by latches attached to her garter belt fastened at her waist. He marveled at the way the silk stockings he brought her, looked and felt as he ran his hand over her lower thigh. But that was nothing compared to the touch of her soft bare yellow skin where the stockings ended. He could hear her breast swishing against the vinyl kitchen chair as he positioned her for penetration. He gently rubbed her bottom as he pushed her skirt higher over the plump and inviting mound to fully expose her vulva. Except for the bald pubic areas he and the all the world had seen in countless paintings and on statues hers was the only one he had seen. But this was the real thing and it was a most beautiful site to behold. Yes, Dalcy had the most beautiful hind parts he could ever imagine seeing in his life. Kennis was so caught up in the moment he decided to kiss it. He had heard about it and if he was ever going to do it, it was now. A long wet and juicy French kiss it was with tongue and all. She quivered so hard at the touch of his lips and tongue on her vulva that she thought she was going to pass out. Her reaction was more than he had anticipated. It was just like Dalcy to intensify the act. At the moment of penetration she shoved her backside toward him and almost knocked him off balance. After their climax they were sure that every neighbor within a miles radius could here them. Then they reassured each other that it wasn't possible because everyone except them was attending the biggest party in Sparks the Annual Cutter's Ball.

For Dalcy his actions were of a most intimate and affectionate nature and it could only mean that he was truly in love with her.

Kennis, on the-other-hand couldn't believe he got so caught up in the moment and that he performed cunnilingus. Damn, what the hell did I do that for? He thought. These are the lips that I kiss my mother on cheek with and Lenora in the mouth. I must wash my lips and than my mouth out with salt water then gargle with rubbing alcohol for at least a week. He supposed that he should be able to kiss Lenora in the mouth again in two weeks or so.

Chapter Twelve
MADELINE'S ADVENTURES

Madeline was blessed beyond measure, yet she was bored almost to tears. Her life of teas, committees, birds and bugs were about to drive her out of her mind. For her nineteenth birthday Madeline was given Miss. Dottie's old one room cabin. It was fixed up and transformed into a workshop complete with microscope, desk, chair, bookshelves, a work table and the old living room sofa. It was more than enough room for her books, notebooks and specimen displays. It was her mother who came up with the idea for the most part to get rid of all the dead bugs as she humorously referred to Madeline's specimens. The bird's nest, bird skeletons, spiders, beetles, worms, chrysalis and butterflies all went to the cabin. Only five of the most beautiful butterfly displays remained in their home. Those kept included three of Madeline's first specimens: the brown and orange American Lady Butterfly (Vanessa virginiensis), which like geese fly south for the winter and the yellow and black Eastern Tiger Swallowtail (Papilio glaucus) and the orange and black Monarch Butterfly (Danaus plexippus). With no electricity she had more than enough light with the many oil lamps she confiscated from various townspeople since most now had electric lights. The heat on cold winter days was provided by the fireplace. Her gift made all of the young women in Kendal Grove envious and gave them someone else to envy for a time instead of Lenora living a grand lifestyle in New York or Patricia being married to Chaz. The workshop was a great blessing she enjoyed but she couldn't remember the last time she had a real deep laugh the kind of laugh you can only have with a bosom buddy. There was something definitely missing. Although, she was very appreciative of her blossoming relationship with Juniper Davis there seemed to be no real fun to be had. Juniper was an avid fan of detective stories those written, performed on the radio or on the screen. No matter how dark or seedy as those written in the pulp fiction magazines, it was good reading to her. She was a bit overweight and not particularly conscious of what she looked good in or what she didn't look good in. Juniper was not quite Madeline's style but she was someone whom she could talk to about more than getting married and having babies. Saturday afternoon matinees featuring detective serials with Juniper broke the monotony for a time but she was beginning to tire of that. When her parents were out on their Friday evening and Saturday afternoon visitations, she and Juniper would turn on the radio, roll back the rug, and practice the latest dance steps. They went ready to swing at the weekend's house parties and dances. But the same people at the house parties and dances were too growing tiresome. If only my mother would let me journey to Parsons to meet other young people or to New York to see Lenora would make for a wonderful and most needed change. The music played on the radio at the ballrooms in Harlem was red hot and swinging. I bet they must really be jumping and jiving to the rhythm of the big bands, she thought. Every so often she pictured her and Lenora dancing at the ballrooms until the sun came up. In her fantasies Chaz and Ricky were there dance partners. Going to New York was strictly in her fantasies because her mother would not hear of it. Being raised in the South, her Mother was afraid to let her out of her site for any length of time. Where her mother was from Negro girls could be kidnapped, raped or murdered at any given time, some never to be seen again. There was no hope for recourse or justice for Negro's.

Just outside of her workshop, Madeline and Juniper would sit on the wooden bench with their backs against the great maple tree for hours. Juniper would secretly hope that a young male stranger would walk up or down the dirt road before them, take one look at her and fall madly in love. Madeline would quietly hope for change, good change. One afternoon, Madeline came up with a plan, so she thought, to evoke change.

It was the first game of the softball season and a month had passed since the plan for change was hatched. Any and everyone wanted to be in attendance at the game. In the bee hive as it was called because it was the Bricktown Yellow Jackets verses the Kendal Grove Hornets. Madeline more than ever looked forward to this game more so than any other game before. This was the chance she had been waiting for to put an end to another boring summer. There had been no real fun for Madeline since Lenora left for New York and Ricky left shortly thereafter to defend the country. Patricia saw to it that there was little communication with Chaz since their marriage with the exception of the monthly Air Raid Warden's meetings in Franklin.

Her excitement was building as she put the finishing touches on her new hairdo. She was finally allowed to get her first permanent wave and it looked great. She turned from one side to the other patting and tucking her curls, viewing herself in the bureau mirror. The long process of straightening her hair with the application of that horrible smelling liquid that burned her scalp was worth the pain after all. It gave her that extra polished edge. Without the new hairdo she turned heads, but with it all the boys from Bricktown as well as the home grown ones would take a long look her way. Not only did she feel good because her hair was freshly done but she also looked great in her brand new outfit. Tan wrap around skirt with a six button short collar orange blouse, brown sandals that fasten at the back of the ankle and a tan scarf tied at the neck. The new look and ensemble gave her the courage to really do the unthinkable. She and Juniper were going to do it this day. They were going to take the left fork instead of the right fork in the pathway and walk across Sassy's parking lot to get to the ball field. They had spied many girls and young women their age walk across the parking lot, lean into the parked cars, and talk to the male occupants. She and Juniper were strictly told never to deviate from the pathway to the right when going to the ball field. They were told to stick to the pathway that led into the seating area surrounding the baseball diamond and to stay away from the pathway that led into the parking lot. But this day, this very day, they were determined to walk across the parking lot and answer to the most promising whistles they received. “Are you ready, Juniper.” asked Madeline. The two young women faced each other, held hands and blurted out at the same time, “You look great!” On this day Juniper had a brand new hairdo as well. She was also outfitted in new attire that complimented her figure for the very first time. They giggled at each other and then hugged before they walked toward the familiar pathway. “There it is!” Juniper said. “Are we really going to do this?” Without answering, Madeline walking on the right side of the pathway gently nudged her friend to the left. Together they veered left on the pathway towards Sassy’s parking lot. The cars were packed in and parked every which way. The smell of sweat and liquor, lots of liquor, permeated their nostrils. The odor was awful, and so unfamiliar to them that they both brought their index fingers under their noses to block the smell. That didn’t last long because their sense of smell was overpowered by the site of the young and good looking male faces from the impoverished Bricktown, a Negro community fifty miles north of Kendal Grove. Not that they were boy crazy but it was nice, really nice, to see the plethora of male faces. They were walking shoulder to shoulder and were about ten feet inside the parking lot before the borage of whistles began. The initial sound of the whistles was so loud that it scared them and they almost embraced. They were basking in the attentions given by their newly found admirers, until they heard their names called. “Madeline, and Juniper, what in the world do you think you are doing?!” Sassy shouted. “As a matter of fact, don’t answer me. I know what you think you’re doing. I advise you to get back onto that pathway and never, I mean never, set foot in this parking lot or anywhere near my place as long as you live on this earth. This is not the kind of place for you, or the kind of company you want to keep! Now get off my property and I don’t ever want to see you come this way again!” The two young women backed away in embarrassment before turning around and making a hasty stride back onto the pathway. When they reached the seating area of the ball field, Madeline’s mother said, “You girls seem out of breath?” “You must have run most of the way to get here on time.” There was no reply from Madeline or Juniper.

Juniper was a good Air Raid Captain under Madeline's direction as was Lippy representing the Hill and Mr. Potts in the Woods under Chaz. A platform and siren were erected adjacent to the parking lot of the general store. At scheduled times, by the air raid committee, the siren would sound and everyone during the day hours would run for cover. At night lights would be extinguished and no smoking was allowed to avoid the community's detection from overhead. From the appointed place, Chaz and Lenora's special place, the wardens and captains could see that all of Kendal Grove was in compliance to the specific instructions of the air raid committee until the "All Clear" was sounded. Lenora in New York was lucky because she got the chance to run into underground subway stations when the alarm sounded, thought Madeline. The children in Kendal Grove were still huddling under their desks or running into dark and damp cellars. Running into a subway station must be exciting? Then she was ashamed of herself for thinking that way, since the people in London were being bombed losing their homes and their lives and the Jews throughout Europe suffered worse.

Change didn't come to Madeline for three more years. But as change sometime does, it came as unwelcome news of the grave illness of her father's Aunt Evelyn. Unwelcome as the news was, it was going to prove to be what she needed in her unadventurous life. She loved her great aunt and very much wanted to spend time with her before she left the living. She knew she was in for the long ride to and from Parsons as well as long hours of visitations in her cramped apartment while there. The second story one bedroom apartment was filled with distant relatives. Kisses, hugs and compliments were given her before an empty plate was placed into her hands to fill. The dining table was filled with all sorts of tasty delights. Before Madeline could make her selections to fill her plate Aunt Evelyn was asking to see her. "Who gets all of the kisses?" Evelyn asked Madeline, as they embraced. "You do Aunt Evelyn," Madeline replied as she showered her aunt's face with kisses before sitting down on her bed.

The gesture lightened the mood and made everyone in her bedroom laugh. From birth Madeline was most preferred of her nieces and nephews, and everyone knew it. Madeline was very attractive, smart, quick witted, kind and neat as a pin. When Aunt Evelyn looked at Madeline it was as if she was looking at her own reflection in her youth. "What have you been up to girly?" Evelyn asked. "Are you still writing to that handsome young man oversees? Someone fix my girly a plate. I want her to eat in here with me." Madeline was about to answer the first question, but couldn't because she was interrupted. "I want the rest of you to go on about your business for awhile, so girly and I can chat." Madeline ate more that Saturday afternoon than was on her plate. She also ate every word spoken from her precious Aunt Evelyn, as somehow she knew these words would be her last. Her aunt was the dearest and wisest person she knew and every word spoken through her lips were like gold. "Girly, I suspect your daddy and your momma will be dragging you to see me every weekend until I leave this world," said Evelyn. "Instead of you coming over here and sitting out there with your greedy, dumb cousins, find something else to do when you come to Parsons. Because ain't a smart one left on this side of the family except for you, your daddy and my son Felix. My other son, Percy, had promise but he married that dumb girl, Justine, and they had dumb children. Stop laughing Girly. Yes they are, dumb as door knobs, every last one of them. Listen here now. I really want you to find something fun to do every time you come to Parsons. It's important for young people to get out and explore things and find new and interesting things to do. As long as it's legal and doesn't hurt anyone, but I don't have to tell you that. Please excuse me child for rambling on and on. I'm accustomed to talking to your dumb cousins. Tell your Momma, Daddy and Felix to come in here. Look ya'll, I want Lenora to ride to Parsons but she doesn't have to sit up in this place. Ya'll drop her at the library before you come see me." How strange, Madeline thought. Her Aunt, looked at her, winked her left eye and smiled. "Felix, reach in my jewelry box, get my silver necklace and bring it over to me," Evelyn went on to say. "Let's put this on you Girly." "Let me see, she said focusing on the jewel necklace around Lenora's neck. "This is from me to you Madeline with much love. Give me a hug, like it's the last one you'll ever give me. Lenora began to sob deeply in the cusp of her great aunt's neck. Evelyn tenderly embraced Madeline and said, "It's alright. If you didn't cry I wouldn't think you loved me. Here, take this too," she said handing Madeline her lace handkerchief. I'll be thinking of you, Girly. I love you." It wasn't until her tears had subsided on the way back to Kendal Grove that Madeline gazed upon the midnight blue "E" embroidered in the right corner of the handkerchief. Aunt Evelyn is so special and was one for always thinking ahead. Madeline had received both something old and something blue. The tears started all over again.

The library was huge compared to Kendal Grove's. Somewhat disinterested Madeline was in no mood to make actual comparisons. She found the sections on birds and bugs, and chose a book from each section before taking a seat at a table to peruse her selections. She noticed two girls around her age one table over from hers. They were in the process of gathering their materials and preparing to leave when she decided to walk over and introduce herself. "Hi, my name is Madeline," she whispered, "can you tell me what kids in Parsons do for fun? "Hi, I'm Jennifer and this is my sister Hazel," Jennifer whispered back, "we go to Sharpy's." "What's Sharpy's?" "It's where we go to have a good time and dance." "You have a place where young people can dance in Parsons." "Yes, it's lots of fun and just a few blocks from here." "Are you going this afternoon?" "We can't go on Saturday's because of our committee meetings. Are you new here?" "No," Madeline answered. She wanted to be polite but didn't want to give away to much information. If her father or mother found that she was anywhere except the library it would be no more Parsons for her. "No, my parents are visiting relatives, and I'm here." "You should go to Sharpy's when you finish here," said Hazel. You seem like a nice girl, I'm sure you would like it and it's not that far." It's out the front door to your left, one block turn left, go right for two blocks, turn right and Sharpy's is on that corner next to the drug store," said Jennifer. Madeline readied her things and followed the girls to the front of the library as far as the checkout desk. "It was very nice meeting both of you, and thanks," Madeline whispered to the girls, waving goodbye. "It was 12:25PM, and she had three hours and thirty-five minutes before her parents would return to pick her up. Using her aunt's address to acquire a library card, she checked her books out, and set off towards Sharpy's.

Sharpy's was like a soda shop out of the movies. Complete with soda fountains, stools, booths, a juke box and space for dancing. It was packed and the kids at Sharpy's knew how to dance. Madeline was sure these kids could only be outdone in their dance steps by the originators of the Lindy Hop in New York. The joint was jittering, hopping, jumping and stomping on this afternoon. "Goodness gracious," she said when the music ended. It was the perfect dance with her sliding through her dance partner's, Bill, legs. Then he pulled her up by both hands with a twist and threw her over his left leg with a hop. Hot you fish! They were right in step. Attending all those Kendal Grove's Friday night house parties and Saturday night dances at the Temple Lodge, and practicing dance steps with Juniper finally paid off, she thought catching her breath and dabbing the perspiration from her neck and face. Bill Sharpy, the son of the owner of Sharpy's was totally taken by his new dance partner. She was a feisty little quick talking and walking baby doll. Standing a little over five feet tall, she was the stuff and had no problem letting one know it. And boy could she dance, over the head, through the legs, jump back and jive. Madeline was aware of his special interest in her but wanted no part of him except as a dance partner. Oh no, where did the time go she thought as she peered at her wristwatch? It was 3:30PM, and it would take her fifteen minutes to return to the library. As soon as Bill turned in another direction, she bolted to the table to get her purse, coat and newly checked-out books before exiting. It was 4:00PM on the dot when her father pulled alongside the curb at the front entrance of Parson's library. "How is Aunt Evelyn," Madeline asked entering the back of the car? "She's doing," replied her Father from the driver's seat. "Did you find any good books," asked her Mother? "Yes, I did mother, two." "That's good, honey." Madeline smiled as she settled back into the seat and gave her Aunt Evelyn a silent, thank you.

While crossing the street on her third visit to Sharpy's she watched as a car slowed down in front of her preparing to make a right turn. In plain view hugging all up under the driver of the car was none other than Patricia. Madeline taking it all in stood motionless and unseen in the crowd awaiting the traffic light to turn green. From her vantage point she could see that the driver was very handsome and looked somewhat familiar. He had one hand on the steering wheel and the other arm wrapped around Patricia. They were smiling and looked happily in love. Carl and Patricia had no idea they were being watched, as they turned the corner heading towards the drug store. "I see you Patricia, girl, and you don't see me," Madeline said to herself, "I wonder if that's her friend or her friend's sick mother." "Be at your best because you never know who's watching," she heard Miss. Dottie say in her mind, "or, what's done in the dark, you can believe, will come to light." Both sayings were appropriate at this moment. Madeline wanted to tell her exactly what was on her mind because her hatred for Patricia was justified and multiplied by ten. "You are a cheat, liar, a back stabber and a..!" She said to herself and stopping short of finishing the name calling. Ashamed for thinking about the last word she could have used to describe Patricia, due to her Kendal Grove upbringing. It was a word often thought about but never used to describe any woman. It started with a "w" and ends with an "e". "That's what you are Patricia!" She thought, exactly what you are! She watched them park the car and enter into the drug store before continuing on her way. She was determined not to let evil thoughts ruin her good time, as she entered Sharpy's. Her dance time of three hours and fifteen minutes was short, so she had to make the best of it.

It was a few weekends of dancing together and nothing more. Bill figured that Madeline's heart was taken by some boy oversees and she was being true to him. She was nothing like the other girls who had someone overseas who were suppose to be madly in love and true. Their boys overseas may be getting the love of their hearts but he was getting from their girlfriends and wives what they couldn't. 4F only meant flat feet for him and he was grateful that everything else worked. He kept himself in great condition to attract the cream of the crop. With the shortage of men there were so many women throwing themselves at him that he had his pick. Choosey, he only picked the pretty and intelligent ones. Overtime his interest in intellect waned, and as long as a woman had full bosoms, a small waist, a nice round and plump bottom, big thighs and a pretty face – she was in. Tall, short, dark, light or in between that was his criteria. Compared to Madeline and her qualities they were all cheap. Given enough time he was sure he could steal her heart away from that soldier boy or who ever and whatever he is. Yep, she had everything a woman should have and he wanted every bit of it. For this one he had to be patient. She was going to be his, he thought.

Since her first visit five Saturday's ago, Bill drove her nuts by constantly trying to manipulate all of her time. He wanted to sit with her and talk and she wanted to dance. Because she was such a good dancer there was no shortage of partners for her. But somehow or another Bill would find a way to cut in. Nonetheless, on this particular cloudy afternoon she was having none of Bill's nonsense and wouldn't allow her partners to let him cut in. She was having a blast so much so that the time had slipped by and she had less than fifteen minutes to get back to the library before her parents got there to pick her up. "Oh, my God," she said peering down at her watch and noting the time. She raced from the dance floor back to her table and on her way out, ran smack into Bill. "Bill, I've got to run," she said frantically. "Run, why do you have to go and where are you going?" he asked. "Look Bill, you can help me with my coat, but I have to go." "Come here girl, wait a minute," he said helping Madeline put on her coat. She wasn't prepared for him pulling her into his arms and looking into her eyes with kindness and genuine concern. "Look, slow down. I'm not going to let you go out in that. It's pouring down rain out there, and you could use a ride. Madeline, let me get my coat and car keys, and I'll take you wherever you want to go. I'm not going to let you get away from me today." Madeline was not one for lying but she had to let Bill think that she would be waiting for him until he returned. "Alright Bill. That's a good idea," she answered. As soon as he was out of her line of sight she exited Sharpy's into the cold pouring rain. It was three blocks back to the library, but with the rain and her time running out the short walk, even as she took quick steps, seemed to take hours. Her shoes were soaked through and if it weren't for the sequestered newspaper from Sharpy's she held over her head her hat, hair and shoulders would be soaked as well. "Good, they aren't here yet," she said to herself as she ran up the library steps without taking a breath. The wet newspaper went into the waste paper basket outside of the library entrance as she hurriedly entered the double doors. Because Madeline had derived a way to maximize her time at Sharpy's she became adapt to selecting new books and checking them out in ten minutes or less. In addition, she would leave her checked books at the library and pick them up from the library in time for her parent's return. At the site of Madeline the Librarian fell into the routine they'd previously established placing her pre-checked books on the counter for her pick-up. A hearty "thank you" was all Madeline could manage to speak as she picked up the books on the edge of the counter, turned and exited the library. They were there, as usual, right on time. The car windows were spotted and streaked with the pouring rain which was to Madeline's advantage. Madeline unbuttoned her coat and tucked the books under her right arm. That's when she noticed that the left side of her dress and slip were wet due to her left arm being extended as she held the newspaper over her head. On the way to the car she tried purposely to step in every puddle she could to avoid any suspicion from her mother as to her wet condition. "Baby you're soaked," said her Mother. "Yes, Mother it's really coming down," she replied. "Where are your books, honey?" Her Father asked. "I have them here, Daddy, under my coat to keep them dry." "Did you get some good ones?" "Yes sir, I got two. "I got one by a scientist who studied entomology in Africa and the other in South America. I wanted compare the two." "That's nice, honey." "Did you send Aunt Evelyn my love?" "Yes we did honey," said her Mother. "Baby, you look like you really got soaked running to the car. Make sure to take a nice hot bath when we get home. Those books look pretty thick. Are you sure you'll finish both by Saturday? "Yes, I plan too." Madeline had no idea that the books would be returned early. Instead of Saturday, the books were returned on Friday before Aunt Evelyn's funeral. It was the end of Madeline's adventures.

Chapter Thirteen
RICKY'S MISSION

Upon news of the declaration of war in the 1941, the older men of Kendal Grove were furious. They despised Chancellor Hitler and the Japanese for what they had begun. The "Trench War," World War I was the war fought to end all wars. They made it back safely to Kendal Grove but from experience they knew it may not be the same for their sons. The many that died and the signing of the Armistead Treaty in 1918 meant absolutely nothing. Forty-eight men from Kendal Grove went off to take part in fighting against the Germans and Japanese. Sixteen of those men were from the graduating class of 1942.

Other than Chaz and Ricky, the other boys graduating in their class hadn't much of a chance for professional opportunities. Chaz was destined to follow in the path of his father and grandfather. Ricky's plan was to work at the store with Mr. Howard, and learn the business with the hopes of owning it. Ricky only shared his closest secret of one day owning the store with those closest to him. Chaz, Lenora and Madeline treated his hopes and dreams like precious gold and had no doubt that in time Ricky would surely make them come to pass. He knew that if he dare share his hopes with anyone else it would be viewed as just another Hill boy's stupid fantasies. Other than military service, the other Hill boys slated to graduate in their class were off to a farm as a farmhand or to the fields as a picker for a lifetime of backbreaking menial labor. Spending long days that stretched into evening, and working your heart out on someone else's farm or in the fields, during any kind of weather, didn't set well with Ricky. Neither did the useless conversations with the under-achieved Hill men that had literally no true value. Or even worse, being assigned to a field where you had to work alongside a picker from Pickers Woods. Ricky wasn't a snob, he wanted to learn and experience the better things in life.

Ricky's first sexual encounter with Patricia was during their senior year, shortly before Lenora's departure to New York. They were together three times in the month of January and twice in the month of February. Ricky experienced a significant element of his ultimate dream for his life. He was madly in love with Patricia and considered their clandestine and fervent moments together as true love and a life long commitment to each other. After all, it was both their first time, they were both Hill children and were the only one's allowed to openly socialize with the residents of Kendal Grove. He had genuine feelings for Patricia, although, unable to express his true feelings or emotions for her or to his best friend, Chaz. She made him vow to never tell a soul of their mutual covert pleasuring before he could kiss or sensually touch her again. "If any of the residents got wind of what they were doing, they'd never speak to us or invite us into their homes again," she said. No one could know what transpired between them because sex before marriage was frowned upon and considered dirty and common. That is except for their little, precious Annie. Ricky, Lenora and Madeline assisted in the wedding preparation. Patricia wasn't included or invited. They were taught that respectable people waited on the sanctity of marriage and were able to control their bodily desires. Unbridled sex was common place on the Hill, in Picker's Woods, but not in the prided residential area of Kendal Grove. Patricia, contrary to Ricky's feelings about her, was only scratching an itch that took root when she haplessly stumbled across Hector Watts and Pickle Johnson huffing, puffing and grunting in the bushes. Pickle, with her out-of-shape, sloppy, ugly self, was on her back with her dress pulled up under her chin and her legs wide open. Watts, as he was referred to by his friends, ugly to the same degree as Pickle, was positioned on top of her between her thighs. His long johns and pants were pulled down around his ankles and his bare bottom moving in a circular motion was exposed to her. Pickle kneaded his back like bread, kissing him and then holding him tightly to her. Despite the sounds of pleasure emanating from them, Pickle's face exhibited pain. Their combined sound made so much noise that they didn't hear her coming up the seldom used pathway. As a matter of fact they didn't notice that someone was watching them. She waited quietly as they finished their business. When done they hurriedly readjusted their clothing and parted without saying a word to each other each going in separate directions. Pickle went up the hill towards her home and Watts went down the hill onto the main pathway towards his home. None would imagine and no one would know what just took place between Pickle and Watts. She knew they were having sex. After all, Kendal Grove was a rural community, and she had witnessed farm animals copulate many times. People weren't supposed to engage until they got married. They weren't married. So, why would she have to wait to experience sex until after she got married? They were holding on to one another as if they never wanted to let go. The sounds they made resounded in her ears. Patricia concluded that what they were doing must feel good, and one day she wanted that good feeling too, after she married Chaz. Puberty, her impatient nature and need for excitement gave way to her wanting to experience what she saw transpire between Pickle and Watts seven years prior in the bushes. She wanted to feel good and she wanted to feel good now. And she knew exactly who would be more than happy to make her feel good for the time being -- Ricky Stone. Oddly, three months and a few weeks before graduation Patricia put a sudden halt to their clandestine meetings that Ricky had become accustomed too. As a matter of fact she cut all forms of communication with him except for succinct topic discussions that took place at school. He wrote it off as one of her mood swings and hoped that it would soon be over. Unbeknown to Ricky her decision to cast him aside was because Lenora was out of the way, and Patricia needed time to concentrate on getting what she thought was her real prize in life… Chaz Carter. Hypnotized by Patricia's tomfoolery, Ricky pictured himself as the town's grocer with this dutiful wife Patricia working by his side. The news of Patricia's pregnancy by none other than his best friend, Chaz, drove him to enlist in the Navy instead. The only thing that came to his mind was the expression "shit or get off the pot" and it was definitely his time to get off the pot. What on earth – O.K. - that's why she stopped – how did they – how could he – Lenora – Patricia – she always wanted him, Chaz – it was never me. Damn! It was Chaz, it was always Chaz, and I planned to marry her. She planned the whole thing. He had to go. He wanted to get as far away from Patricia and Kendal Grove as he could.

After the heroic accomplishments of a Negro Mess Man at Pearl Harbor, other military occupations were beginning to open to Negro's in the segregated armed forces. Not in the mood to be put on a waiting list until other military occupations were made available, to accept his high test scores, he selected Mess Man. He figured now was the time to leave and he'd rather cook than shine another man's shoes. He left for boot camp two weeks after their June 3rd graduation date.

On the long bus ride to boot camp were intellectuals, loud mouths, thieves, cut throats, and pretenders. Ricky knew to keep to himself to avoid any asinine confrontations. It was as if he was watching some kind of show, a play, as he watched the many personalities unfold before him. He had no complaints because it created a great diversion from his thoughts about Patricia. When the main gate of the base came into view the chatter ceased all at once. Ricky too looked goggle-eyed at the sharply dressed MP's stationed at the gate. Dressed in all white with white helmets, shinny black combat boots and hand-held automatic weapons holstered in their gun belts was a novelty. A man, sharply dressed as the MP's with a clip board, boarded the bus before it was permitted through the gate by a sharp wave of the MP. "Listen up!" he shouted. "Good morning you fagots, I am Sergeant Fricket, and until somebody feels sorry enough about your sorry asses to pick you up, you'll be dealing with me! You will meet your other instructors when we reach our destination!" A few of the guys on the bus blurted out questions. "What?!" said the Sergeant. "Shut up! I don't care if you have any questions. Momentarily you are here to listen and not talk, so do so!" Negro recruits were stationed at the far northern end of the base, and in addition to the MP's there was lots more to see on the way. He saw the base hotel, hospital, quonset huts, parade decks, non commissioned officers club, officers club, a golf course, PT boats, ships and finally a submarine before reaching their destination. "Listen up! Fricket barked. "You have arrived at your new home for the next six weeks! When you get off the bus make a straight line along the yellow line! Move it, move it!" When the line was complete he went on to say, there are four platoons in a division, eight barracks and sixty men to each barrack. "Two units or barracks make a platoon. I will call your name and assign your barracks and your serial number," said Fricket. "You will meet your instructors on the inside and if your dumb asses have questions than ask them! Stone, Ricky, Platoon 320, Unit A, serial number 329858." The barracks were no more than forty-by-forty feet with four out side to outside walled structures, on six brick piers, plank floors, six double hung windows with a shingled pitched roof. Only a carpenter or the son of a carpenter would notice straightaway. The interior had three distinct areas, the drill instructors office, the open squad bay and the bathroom which was referred to as the "head." His rack, not bunk as in the army, had an upper and a lower. He was assigned the upper that was located one rack over from the drill instructors hut. There were 30 racks on one side and 30 racks on the other side. The barking from the drill instructors at first seemed completely unnecessary until he ascertained, within a few short hours, the lack of discipline and coordination demonstrated by his fellow recruits. With the idiosyncrasies of sixty young men thrown together and the merciless barking of the Drill Instructors, Ricky prayed and hoped for the best. Hair cuts, bed linens and basic equipment issue were up next. One pillow, one pillow case, one blanket, two sheets were issued. One duffel bag, two light blue utility shirts, two pairs of utility blue jeans, one jacket, two white sailor covers, one belt, one pair of deck shoes, one pair of combat boots, two sets of athletic clothing and one rifle. The bullets were not included and that was a good thing. "Some of you assholes are wondering why you don't have a uniform!" The Drill Instructor yelled. Aren't you?! Have you done a damn thing to deserve a uniform?! Uniforms are only issued after you prove that you are good enough to be in my great Navy! And some of you will be sent home crying before I see you in my uniform! Do you hear me?!" Platoon A responded in unison, "Yes sir!" It had been a long day and it was only the beginning of many long days to follow. Each morning they would awake at 5:00AM. Be on line in front of their racks by 5:02AM, be back on line in front of their made racks and dressed at 5:20AM. All hands were on deck and ready for inspection before the march to "chow" which was the word used for each meal of the day. Physical training, naval history, educational training, drilling, hand-to-hand combat training, swabbing, inspections, swimming, rowing and shooting was what he had to look forward to for the next six weeks. That evening at lights out the Drill Instructor had an earful for the faint at heart. "I've got a little present for you queers," he said. "Tomorrow is the special day set aside to meet our special medical team. Shots are on the agenda, a whole lot of shots! That is needles! Goodnight ladies." Ricky thought he heard whimpers coming from several racks within the barracks but shrugged it off as his imagination.

All he had to do is put all the information to memory and execute the commands when ordered. Attention, dress-right-dress, forward-march, left-right-left, platoon halt, fall out, fall in, ey ey sir. There were easier things to remember like the names of the President, Vice President, Secretary of State or Secretary of the Navy. Specific information taught also had to be retained, such as: When was the first American Navy established? Who was the first Admiral of the Navy? Who was the first Secretary of the Navy? In what year were they appointed?

Stanton, Vincent Stanton was the one Ricky had to beat. The boy from the city had a slight edge on Ricky. Stanton received Out Standings on the first two Inspection Reports, while Ricky received Satisfactory on his. Stanton had boot camp down pact because his two older brothers had gone through the process months prior and wrote to him details for success in basic training. The slight edge from Stanton's brothers wasn't the issue. Ricky tried but couldn't identify the difference between the two whether on line, rack or locker box inspections. Then one day Ricky noticed Stanton did have a little extra that he didn't possess. It was simply, "snap-to-it-ness." Ha, I got it! He thought. Ricky had respect for those in authority over him and he was accustomed to it because that's the way he was raised. The barking out of orders, jumping up to attention and not looking people straight in the eye, when you spoke to them or were spoken to, was altogether new to him. Like everything else with Ricky Stone, once he got it, he got it. Boot Camp was a breeze after the revelation. It was he and Stanton neck and neck but Ricky excelled and took the lead when it came to physical training and intellectual testing. Ricky scored at the top of the entire division in math, English and general knowledge. At the rifle range he scored the highest in the division as Sharp Shooter. "In war you don't shoot to wound," the Instructor said. "You shoot to kill or you will be killed." Ricky only needed to hear that once, he had no inkling about being killed. Scoring at the top in every area of training, he was the first recommended for E-2 Meritorious Seaman Apprentice and Stanton came second. Only three meritorious promotions were awarded the division.

His orders specified he would be sailing the South Seas. His destination was undisclosed. From boot camp he reported to his duty station the U.S.S. Celestial a light aircraft carrier. A tour of a ship during boot camp was one thing but to actually live on one was indescribable. "This is really happening to me," he thought. The Celestial was a beauty from stern to aft. He put his duffel bag down, stood at attention and saluted the Quartermaster at the edge of the gang plank. "Stone, Ricky, 329858, reporting for duty sir," he said. The Quartermaster returned his salute and allowed him access to the gang plank. At the top of the gang plank he again put his duffel bag down before saluting the United States Flag of America flying high above the ship. Then he saluted the Captain before requesting permission to board the ship. Once aboard ship he repeated his name and serial number before being directed to his quarters.

Through the narrow passage ways, hatches and stairwells of the ship he went. Five decks below to the aft of the ship and to the starboard side he reached his quarters. All of the sixty men of color were bunked in the same squad bay area which was similar to boot camp but much tighter. Ricky was the first of the fresh graduates to arrive on the ship. The others, including Stanton, were out site seeing around the base. At least, the area they weren't restricted from. Ricky preferred to get acquainted with his new surroundings aboard ship before the others arrived. He lucked out and found one empty mid-level rack in the Negro crew's compartment that was far enough away from the main traffic going and coming from the head and the hatch. The other unoccupied racks were located on the top. The first and second levels of the racks were a tight squeeze. At the top your face was so close to the ceiling that it was as if you were in a steal coffin and Ricky wanted none of that.

The ship sailed from the Atlantic Ocean to the Pacific Ocean to his first port of call in San Francisco, California and then it was off to sea. He was fascinated by the dark blue inky color of the deep sea and the transparent waters of the South Seas. Depending on where you were the color of the body of water could be blue, pale green or turquoise. The sea birds, albatrosses, pelicans and gulls, diving and scooping up fish for supper were a constant source of amusement. He wondered what Reverend Joe would think if he brought one of the birds home with him? There would certainly be no need for fishing poles on the annual fishing trip. That's for sure. Like clockwork he wrote Madeline twice weekly. Notating the date and time of day each letter was written. His location somewhere in the South Seas, however, was omitted for the sake of secrecy. On some evenings from the flight deck Ricky would take in Gods magnificent play. Seeing the sun, the glorious sun, go down with a backdrop of purple, yellow, brown, beige and orange. It was like watching a gigantic horizontal curtain close the day. For millions of years an act untouched by man. The only thing missing was Madeline at his side. Or after the sun had set he would stand on the flight deck with his feet firmly planted and feel the wind braking across his chest and the inertia of the ships movement. It solidified his existence. Little Ricky Stone from Kendal Grove was somebody somewhere in the South Pacific. He existed.

The kettles filled with the great tasting morsels at Camp Meeting were big but those pots and kettles didn't compare to the size of those on board ship. Boy was he glad that he learned cleanliness at an early age because in the military cleanliness was the way of life. Rank was easily obtained by Ricky he found solace in the most minuscule of duty assignments. Meritorious Seaman First Class was awarded to him in boot camp. After boot camp graduation the rank of E-3 Seaman and E-4 Petty Officer 3rd Class quickly followed. While serving on USS Celestial in the South Pacific he saw plenty of action and he saw the results of it. His ship alone had been hit by enemy fire twice and each time brought about casualties. He had seen both dead and heavily wounded on his ship, enough to make him avoid hospitals for the rest of his life. Little Ricky Stone had traveled half the world over water. He wasn't one to go ashore often except to buy trinkets for loved ones at home. While other guys ate it up, the lore of easy women and fast talking hucksters weren't found the least bit attractive. Other than his crewmates and best buddies Stanton, Summerfield and Sovell his only other release were letters from Madeline and fond memories of Kendal Grove. Not that the other letters from Kendal Grove didn't matter, Madeline's letter made him recognize and appreciate being alive.

Ricky was outside on the third deck peeling potatoes for what he was sure was the one hundred millionth time. He had peeled so many potatoes that his hands and fingers had long since stopped shaking, aching and cramping. He could have assigned someone lower in rank for the duty but he found it therapeutic. Though the ship was large there was little privacy. Each space was filled almost to capacity with crewmen or officers all trying to get their points across. There was no time for thinking or anything else other than reacting on command. For this particular duty of peeling potatoes it only took two or three personnel to perform. If he had enlisted in June instead of May he may have been given the opportunity to choose another military occupation other than mess. He might have chosen to work as a flight deck crewman giving the thumbs up to launch aircraft. He thoroughly enjoyed participating in the "Boardwalk" clearing the flight deck of any debris for clear takeoffs when he could. Or maybe he would have continued his education and taken night college courses and attended Officer's Training School. If that was the case then he would have chosen to be up in "Vulture's Row" overlooking and coordinating the flight deck and have access to the ready room like the officers. As it stood he was responsible for the mess duty roster and when he peeled potatoes the other one or two assigned with him were the most unspoken of the bunch. Early on in his assignment he had the duty with Stanton and Summerfield. There was so much laughter, talking and cutting-up that very few potatoes were peeled among them. Their poor performance got them written up and two months of garbage detail. Today between the three of them there was no chatter other than the sound of the ship making passage across the water. Stanton said that he understood why ships and boats were named after women. "Listen," he would say, "ships and boats moan, hem and haw. And when they get older it becomes louder and then begins to creak. Wait, listen. Hear that? Just like a woman!" He said, twisting his lips to one side, and clapping his hands together to illustrate his point.

Ricky agreed that a ship makes many sounds but this particular sound reminded him not of a woman. The sound reminded him of a warm and cloudy Sunday afternoon in Kendal Grove on the Hill. He was about seven years old when Mr. and Mrs. Potts came up the Hill in their rickety wagon. Something was wrong with the wagon from the sound of metal scraping coming from the undercarriage. The horse pulling the wagon looked as if it was going to drop dead after the trek up the hill. There they were sitting atop the wagon totally oblivious to the people drawn to the noisy wagon stopping at the Stone house. "Woe dare, Tricksta," Mr. Potts called out to his horse. "Lil boy, dare." "Yes sir," Ricky answered. "Is dis be the home of Macabee Stone?" "Yes sir, it is." "Is he home?" "Yes sir, he is." Not looking back at his wife Potts jumped from the wagon then picked up his double barreled shotgun. Again, he faced the little boy and said, "Tell em, com on out eir cause somebody wants to see em." Potts had a fearsome reputation, but had never been a threat to Ricky. He was familiar with the man from his church attendance, and visits to Annie at the edge of the lane to Picker's Woods. This time was different because in front of him and his home stood the man with his infamous double barreled shot gun in-hand. The man who would shoot you down, like a rabbit dog if you crossed him or his kin. Ricky froze in place from fear and could not move one inch. He didn't have to because behind him Macabee was coming through the screen door. His father, a man of few words, gently reached down and placed his open hand in the center of his son's chest and said, "Go inside boy, and move away from the screen door." That was when Ricky heard the crowd murmur and noticed the two scarred, bruised and swollen faced young men chuckling in the midst of the crowd. It was Phillip and Alec, Annie's brothers, at the front of the crowd that assembled across the road from Macabee Stone's house. "Is u Macabee Stone," asked Potts. "Yes. That's me," said Macabee stepping to the edge of his front porch. It was a warm day and Macabee had opened the front door and all of the windows in their house to allow in fresh air. This gave Ricky the advantage to peer out of the kitchen window and be in ear shot of what was taking place in the front of his home. "My boys sa u beat da tar out em?" "Yes, I did," answered Macabee. "One of em sa he smack a gal cause she sa dae dirty and dae stink. Den de ova one smack er. Den er brova jump n and try ta stop em. Den das beat em down. Dat win u jump in and beat de tar out boff of dem." Macabee answered, "yes that's about how it went." The next action flabbergasted all of Kendal Grove. With his infamous double barreled shotgun in his left hand Potts stepped forward and extended his right hand to Macabee. Macabee took his right hand into his own, it was a real handshake. Both men shook firm and confident with neither trying to overpower the other. Then Potts uttered his next words so all could hear, "Thank you. My boys was taut ta b beda den dat. Don no Potts man go round beaten no gal. Dae stink and dae dirty. Dat gal was rite. Come on yea, Alec n Phil, git on up to dis wagon." Alec and Phillip hadn't moved a muscle since their father said of all things, "thank you." They had no choice except to obey. The embarrassment from the crowd was nothing compared to the fear of what their father would do to them. Off they went back down the Hill with the wagon sounding of the grinding metal. A few of the men that were in the crowd came to the property line of the Stone house to tout their favor of Macabee's unflappable demeanor. They knew not to enter the yard unless they were asked too, and none asked because they knew they'd be refused. "Macabee, you sure got the right last name, cause don't nothing bother you," one of them said. "You're like a stone that has been stuck in the ground since the beginning of time," another man said. Initially he didn't respond. Then he looked in their direction, shook his head and said, "Ya'll go on about your business." Ricky was astounded by his father's lack of fear. There had been a man in front of their house, who had a double barreled shotgun and then as now Macabee seemed undaunted as he sat down in his arm chair. He smiled, shook his head, looked at his son and asked, "Were you scared, boy?" "Yes sir," Ricky answered. "There was no need to be scared. No sane man is going to shoot another man in front of his wife. What I've heard about Potts is he's a fair and hard working man that takes care of his family. He is very much like me, because he doesn't talk a lot and don't believe in putting on no show. He's a doer. Those two young sons of his, they're wild, but I bet they don't carry-on like that around their Pa and Ma. From the looks on their faces when they got into that wagon they probably won't carry on like that again." Macabee looked sullen when he said, "It's stupid and below any man to hit a woman. I know that now." He added, "Never hit a woman, Ricky. And never put any woman, you love, in a state where she would want to hit you. I know that now," he repeated.

Night had fallen and he was coming to the last of the potatoes to be peeled for tomorrow mornings hash browns. He was on the next to his last potato to peel when he decided to ask Madeline to be his wife. He looked upward at the stars and realized that his buddies had been dismissed for twenty-four hour shore leave about two hours ago. He laughed to himself because he knew that the girl, the "it girl," all his shipmates were searching for was what he had waiting for him at home. Madeline was a thoughtful, smart, shapely, feisty and witty girl. As true as true could be. He didn't have to worry about anyone beating his time. The only thing she feared was God. She often said that God was the only thing that kept her in line. She was also a great cook and neat as a pin. She was also the right height for him. Without her heels she came just below his chin. He longed again to look down into her big brown eyes and kiss her forehead, the tip of her nose and than her soft full lips. He'd never kissed her lips before. Was she the color of coffee with a table spoon of cream or the color of dark caramel candy? It really didn't matter because he loved his coffee that way, he loved caramel candy and he loved Madeline. No other woman could replace her and he didn't want to waste anymore of his time constantly comparing other women to her. She was right under his nose all of his life and it took a war for him to recognize what a prize she was.

"She'll be wearing a navy blue suit, navy blue hat with white ribbon, and blue shoes," said Ricky. That's what Ricky's life long friend would be wearing when she met him at the docking station in New York. "What are you repeating to yourself, man?" Stanton asked. "My childhood friend, Lenora, is meeting us this afternoon when we disembark and that's what she said she'd be wearing," answered Ricky. "We'll help you look for her man." "What are we looking for, a Lena Horn, Pearl Bailey or Hattie McDaniel?" Sovell asked putting on his finishing touches before standing on line for dismissal. They had a forty-eight hour pass for leave in New York City, New York and he and his shipmates were on their way to Harlem escorted by Lenora. On the port station the questioning began again. "Man, what does she look like?" asked Summerfield. "Give us the low down on her." "Well, she's ah," Ricky couldn't find the right words to describe his good friend. "Ah what man? What's the hold-up?" "Well, ah, she's about 5'5" and studying to be a teacher." "A teacher, so we're not looking for a hot doll, pin-up girl type? Stone, are you trying to tell us we'll be escorted by a schoolmarm?" asked Stanton. "Well, she's a lot of fun and I am sure she will know, or can tell us what to do." "Man are you tying to tell us that tea, real tea may be involved with this chick?" "Well ah, yea." "Oh man, what have you gotten us into?" "The last thing any of us are thinking about is setting around drinking tea with a schoolmarm and a bunch of old ladies." "I tell you what, if things get too dull, you all can take off." "That's a great idea," said Stanton. "What's the signal for go, we are gone, outta here," asked Summerfield. "I'll say, Miss., thank you for the invitation, but we've made other plans," said Stanton. "That will mean let's run!" "Sounds good," they all agreed of course except, Ricky.

There were hundreds of people waiting for their loved ones all hugging, kissing, laughing and crying. Ricky and his shipmates looked around through the crowd aguishly for a Negro woman dressed like a schoolmarm. It was than that Summerfield hunched Ricky and said, "Man oh man, look what's coming this way. It's too bad that's not her." The four of them were stuck in their tracks as they watched the most beautiful and elegant dark skinned woman any of them had ever seen walking in their direction. Her suit was tailored to fit her hour glass figure. The four buttons down the front, square shouldered jacket had a square collar and the sleeves were cuffed with a button at each cuff. The slim waist skirt stopped three inches below her knees exposed beautifully shaped legs. Her shoes were blue, two inch, leather round toed platform pumps. Her blue leather purse strap was slung over her left shoulder and her left forearm rested on the top of it. Her hat with a big white bow in the front set slightly tilted to the right in a nest of curls. Her eyebrows were arched and accented bedroom eyes with clear whites surrounding her ebony irises. Her teeth were sparkling white as they shown through her full lips turned up into an inviting smile. "Hey fellow she's coming this way," said Stanton. No one noticed that her suite was navy blue and she was wearing a blue hat with a white bow. Then as if awakened from a dream, the face coming towards him was familiar. It looked like but couldn't be Miss. Lethea. Miss. Lethea had been dead for many years and this woman looked familiar but was all together different. "This woman was more beautiful, and oh, my God, this woman was, no it couldn't be, it's Lenora!" he said to himself with great surprise. Ricky ran to her and grabbed her up into his arms. When he put her down he cupped her face into his hands and proceeded to kiss every part of her face. They laughed and hugged at least four more times before they let go of one another. "I didn't know it was you, I didn't know it was you," he said again and again as he held her at arms length. "It's me, Ricky Stone," she said. You have grown up from a little scrawny boy to a big strong sailor man." Ricky's shipmates stepping all over each other finally made their way over to the beautiful Lenora. Each one impatiently waited, with hat in hand, for an introduction. "Gentlemen, I would like to introduce you to one of my oldest and closest friends, who is also my sweetheart's best friend, Miss. Lenora Howard." They hurriedly introduced themselves one-by-one. "It's a pleasure to meet each of you," said Lenora. Please follow me this way gentlemen, she said extending her right forearm in the direction of the street exit. "My Lenora all grown up," said Ricky as Lenora led the way to the cab stand. "You think she might invite us to tea?" whispered Stanton to Summerfield. "I hope so man, I hope so," replied Summerfield. "Forget the tea cups, I'll drink tea out of her shoe," said Sovell.

Lenora and Ricky were discussing the highlights of the previous night during an early dinner when a frantic knock and ringing of the bell came at the door. "Yes he is, gentlemen," said Lizzy answering the door. "May I have your names, gentleman? Please come this way," she said leading Ricky's shipmates to the dining room to announce their arrival. Ricky removed the napkin from his lap, wiped his mouth and stood to greet them. Before he could speak Summerfield said, "Excuse me Lenora. Do you live here?" "Yes, I do," she replied. He whistled as he and the others looked around admiring the opulence. "Hey, take a look at the proper fellow," he said referring to Ricky's mannerisms when they entered the room. "Did you see what he did when we came in? It was all in one move." "Yep, a proper fellow, a proper fellow indeed," said Sovell elbowing Stanton in his ribs. "We didn't know you lived like this, Stone." "I don't, yet, but I hope to some day." "There's nothing wrong with that, there's nothing wrong with that," Stanton repeated. "What's going on fellows?" asked Ricky. "You weren't due here until 2000. That is 8:00PM your time, Lenora." "We've gotten word that we are pulling out tonight, and have to be back to the ship by 2000." "What!" Ricky said almost in a state of panic. "The plan was set and it was an accurate plan." "Don't worry," said Lenora. "You'll be cutting it close, but you can make the telephone call one hour earlier. That will give you ten minutes to talk and the time needed to get back to the ship." "What call?" asked Stanton, "and what plan?" Lenora looked at Ricky to gain permission to share. He gave her a solemn nod in favor of sharing their plan. "He is proposing to Madeline this evening by telephone." "Wait, what, tonight, and you didn't tell us?" "No, I was waiting to tell you after we had shoved off tonight." "O.k., run this plan by us," said Sovell. "Let's go into the drawing room, and he'll explain," said Lenora. The sailors were in awe of Lenora's home that is except for Ricky. Who was no longer as awed since he had spent what was left of the night before and the whole of the day in the comforts of his friends New York home.

They were all seated as Ricky began divulging the plan. "I wrote to Madeline's father at the funeral home where he works over four months ago to inform him of my intentions. He responded with his blessing. Last month, Lenora and I set this plan in motion after we learned I would be granted leave in New York." His shipmates were leaned forward on the edge of their seats. Ricky continued, "I bought the engagement ring a month ago on shore leave, and mailed it to her father. Tonight Madeline's parents are hosting our engagement party disguised as a pot luck supper. Those invited are my best friend, Chaz, his parents and grandfather." Lenora lowered her head, ever so slightly, when Chaz' name was mentioned. It was a name she hadn't heard or spoke of in over three years, but the feelings were still there. Ricky went on to say, "Lenora's family will be there and a good friend of Madeline's. I was supposed to make the telephone call after dinner during coffee and dessert. Now I'll have to make the call before they sit down to dinner. And who knows about Madeline's whereabouts? She could be off anywhere chasing birds or bugs." The fellows gave each other puzzling looks. Ricky feeling helpless said, "Lenora, you know she's always running late for dinner." The fellows didn't know what to think because nothing unnerved Stone. Lenora in her delicate way placed her hand on her friend's shoulder to assure him all would work out fine.

The doorbell rang and to Lenora's surprise it was Kennis whom she hadn't seen in over two weeks. In addition, he came unannounced. She figured the word had gotten out that she was seen around town with four unknown to the Circle service men. She was more right than she knew. Not only did Kennis hear the exact same thing, but he was out to make damn sure that no other man was going to beat his time and leave a mark on his territory. He had spent too much time, money and energy on her. Lenora was patriotic and sweet, with a heart of gold. No other man was going to tell her some sob story and wiggle his way between her legs before he did. He was the only man in her life and he intended for it to remain that way. He hadn't heard the name Chaz in years and as far as he was concerned there was no room for conversation about any other man except him, which meant no mention of her father, either. "Kennis what a surprise," said Lenora upon seeing him. He took the liberty to embrace and kiss her cheek to indicate their close relationship. His advances made her uncomfortable, because she knew Kennis didn't believe in openly expressing affection. She introduced her guests saving Ricky for last. One of the dumb ass hillbillies made there way to the big city, Kennis thought shaking Ricky's hand. "Yes darling, I remember you mentioning him," Kennis said. Ricky had thoughts about Kennis too but they were more in line with the truth. Look at this lazy, spoiled, flat footed ass that shakes hands like a girl and gets by on his looks and father's money, Ricky thought. There most likely isn't a compassionate bone in his body and if he didn't have flat feet he would have found another way not to participate in the war. I wonder if he knows Lenora wrote to me and told me of his flat feet. I didn't like him when she first wrote me about him and I really don't like him now that I've met him. Kennis sat down, removed his solid gold cigarette case from his breast pocket and removed a cigarette from it. He really didn't want to offer the others one, but it was the polite thing to do. He really got a kick out of Vincent, Huey and Jeffrey ogling his every move. "Is that real gold?" asked Huey with his mouth wide open and his eyes bulging out like one of the Negro comedians in the movies. "Yes, it is solid gold," answered Kennis. After rummaging around in is jacket pocket for a few seconds, he said. "And here is the lighter that matches. My father gave it to me on my twenty-first birthday." "Boy," exclaimed Huey, "I bet that set him back a bit." "No not at all," said Kennis as he toyed with the slender lighter between his long manicured fingers. He knew that they were impressed with his every movement. He comfortably leaned back into the arm chair next to the fireplace with his right leg crossed over his left, swinging his right foot. Look at them eating up everything I say and do, he thought. "I still embody the word "debonair" like the anonymous admirer quoted in my college brag book, if I must say so myself," Kennis sat talking and amusing himself until he looked in the direction of Ricky. All he saw was what looked like disgust. Why, the nerve – what – why that is disgust, he thought sitting erect, how dare him? "Watch me put him in his place," he said to himself. "So, Ricky that is your name, isn't it?" "Yes. That's right," Ricky answered. "So Ricky, what is it that you do on that big ship? "I am a Mess Man." "You mean you are…a cook?" "I guess, you could say that." "Don't you get tired of peeling all of those potatoes, washing all those pots, pans and such?" "Of course I do, but it beats sitting around all day and doing nothing except going to tea parties and night clubs." The fellows knew precisely what was going on and decided to sit back and watch Stone handle his business. They knew Kennis was in for a verbal bout and Ricky Stone was going to win. Under the premise that bucks from Kendal Grove, with the exceptions of Lenora's father, were dimwitted field hands, Kennis was embarrassed. There was nothing wrong with his lifestyle of plenty. Why should he feel anything other than dignified? After all, Ricky was only a cook and no less a glorified one. By-the-way, his family hired and fired cooks. "I really don't understand why you need a uniform to cook, because it's really not like you're helping the war effort." "Kennis, is it? You would think that way, because you are not involved in the war effort." "I have you know my father landed a very large contract to manufacture shoes for the military," Kennis said heatedly. "What has that got to do with you, Kennis? "You see, without food and nourishment there would be no allied forces. Without substances, such as in food, one cannot live. That is food carefully and skillfully prepared by cooks like me." The verbal bout was over due to the expression on Kennis' face and Stone once again was the victor. Kennis could feel his chin touch his jacket collar. He found in a most unprecedented way that Ricky Stone was no dumb, country field hand. He had no choice but to make an excuse and speedily departed to escape more embarrassment. "Lenora I'll take my leave," he said. "I stopped by on my way to a pressing engagement. There is no need to ring for Henry or Lizzy, I'll show myself out." After retrieving and donning his hat and overcoat he angrily rushed out the front door. It was than he came to the realization that he hadn't accomplished one thing that he set out to do. The first was to break-up Lenora's little party and send the little service boys shamelessly back to their ship after taking one look at him. It was known that most people in his presence, no matter their station in life, felt outclassed by his impeccable good looks, demeanor and wit. The second was to ask Lenora out to dinner on the following evening. He had failed at both attempts. He wanted to get back at her for not throwing herself at his feet when he arrived. After all, she hadn't had the pleasure of his company for almost three weeks. In addition, she didn't rush to his aide when Ricky criticized his way of life. To bolster his spirits; he was going to Dalcy's tomorrow evening instead. But from hereafter, he was only going to kiss the lips on Dalcy's face.

Ricky was glad that Kennis was gone. In no way did he want him to be a part of this special evening. It was time to make the telephone call. The ring at the other end of the call was not completed before the receiver was picked up. "Mr. Trusdale," said Ricky. "Yes son," he answered. "I would like to ask you for your daughter, Madeline's hand in marriage." "Yes, you may, and may God bless you." "Madeline," her father called beckoning her to the telephone. Baffled, Madeline answered, "Yes, Father?" "This telephone call is for you," he said handing her the receiver. "It is, who on earth is telephoning me?" Taking the receiver from her father's hand, she looked around at the actions and expressions exhibited by her parents and guests. The married couples were holding one another. Chaz and Reverend Joe were smiling, as if that was the only thing they were born to do and Juniper looked as if she couldn't decide whether to go to the bathroom or cry. "Hello, Madeline." "Yes." "It's Ricky." "Oh, it's Ricky, everyone," she exclaimed broadly smiling. "I'm here in New York with Lenora." "Ricky you are, really? How are you, how is she?" "We're fine, we both are fine, but it's something I really want to ask you." "Alright, Ricky, I'm so happy to hear your voice, what is it?" Madeline's father moved closer to her. Nervous, she again asked, "Ricky what is it?" "Madeline Trusdale, will you marry me?" Her father presented and opened the small jewel box, he held behind his back, before her. Inside was a gold solitaire engagement ring. With her left hand cupped over her face and her right holding the receiver, she uttered loudly, "Yes!" "She said, yes," Ricky yelled out on Lenora's telephone. Screams, hugs, kisses, hand shaking and back slapping went all around at both ends of the telephone line. Ricky's shipmates couldn't make up their minds which they were most happy about, congratulating Ricky or kissing Lenora. "I love you, I love you Madeline, and I can't wait for you to be my wife. I have to go. It was wonderful hearing your voice. Tell everyone that I said, hello. I'll be home before you know it. Take care, darling." Ricky left the home of Lenora's grandmother with three thoughts. The first being how lucky and proud he was to be engaged to the likes of Miss. Madeline Trusdale. Secondly, what a wonderful time he had in New York with one of his oldest and dearest friends, Lenora. And thirdly, what a rich, silly, selfish and lazy fop Kennis Beavin was.

Within a few months after his proposal to Madeline the war was over and Ricky had seven months remaining of his tour of duty. Seven months until he could return home to Kendal Grove where he planned to live out the rest of his days. He had earned his place around the old pot belly stove at the general store with the other veterans reliving his ruritan tales.

At the request of Reverend Joe, Ricky had to make one stop before he went home. He had to make a visit to some very close friends of the Carter family. Because the request was made by Reverend Joe, Ricky was more than happy to oblige.

Chapter Fourteen
SONNY'S GET AWAY

Any reason was a good enough reason for Sonny Jordon to get away from his wife Annie and their four children for the ride to Parsons to see his woman, Grace. There was not a place in the world like Toby's where he met Grace. Sassy's little juke-joint in Kendal Grove could never compare. The drunks that hang-out there would flip if they ever stepped into Toby's. It was more than not being served watered down drinks in canning jars or the tables and chairs not matching. At Toby's the walls were covered with red fuzzy wallpaper and over the bar hug a large mirror in a gold frame with Toby's written across it, in big black letters, and the floor in the seating area was covered in red carpet. The barstools were covered in leather with the same color red to match the walls. The wood around the bar, the stools, tables and chairs was dark cherry and polished to a high gloss. There was a stage for entertainment and plenty of room for dancing. Of all the times he had gone to Toby's not once had he seen a couple argue or come to blows. At Sassy's on an average of two or three times a week a fight would break out. They didn't need live entertainment because they had each other. The women at Toby's were also better looking. They walked, talked and acted better plus they really knew how to treat a man. These women also had the figures to go with their looks, and Grace, his woman, was the best of them all. Sonny knew Grace was four to six years older then he but he didn't mind because she was fine. No matter which night he stopped by Toby's she was there waiting for him and looking good. Her smiling face was round and pretty. Her skin was without blemish and she kept the fingernails on her velvety soft hands painted. Her hair was meticulously kept, except when they made love. And all of her smelled of fresh flowers which wasn't noticeable unless you got up real close on her, which was the place he desired to be day and night. Grace was his woman, neat and clean, the same way she kept her place. Not like Annie, his wife, who was fairly nice looking, neat enough, but looked tired and worn out most of the time. One of the reasons he was so crazy about Grace was they could dance all night long, every night. After dancing, he'd go to her place for a few more drinks, a good meal and a bit of good loving. Then hit the road again. Sonny loved being a trucker for Cornwell's Fuel, as well as he loved his life. The only downside he felt was his wife Annie and their children. He never wished any harm come to them but he would rather be with Grace. If Annie would let me go, he thought, I could really be happy. He wanted no more talks with Reverend's Joe or James Carter about the responsibility of a married man with children according the Good Book. Nor did he want anymore sideways looks from folks in Kendal Grove, or hear Daddy this or Daddy that. He wanted no more Annie, her church folks or their boys!

Life was good with Grace. He liked spending time at her place with her mother Ida and Ida's man, Black. Black was a loud, burley, dark, cigar smoking man who had a good heart and would give his life for Ida and Grace. He often teased Grace by saying, "Girl, I have been around you and your Momma so long, you should have been my daughter." Grace would hunch Black in the side with her elbow and say, "Nah uh, because while you were trying to get to Momma the milk man beat you too it. Didn't Momma ever tell you that the milk man was my daddy?" "You'd better go on girl," Ida would say while Black, Grace and Sonny roared in laughter. "Ya'll, laughing at me are ya? That's why you will get no gingerbread tonight after dinner." "We just kidding around, Miss. Ida," said Black. "If I had ever had the tiniest notion that the milk man was trying to get my stuff, I would have whipped his skinny tail and went to jail for it. You know what, Ida? I used to see him look awful close at you when your back was turned." "So, why didn't you say something then Black?" Ida asked. "Aw girl, there was no real harm in looking, and I didn't want to mess up your milk service. You had a new baby, and you couldn't do no milking yourself because you're afraid of cows, and." "Don't you say another word Black," she interrupted. "I don't want to hear no more come out your mouth," she said placing her hand over his mouth. "No, Momma, let him talk." Grace said pulling her mother's hand away from his mouth. "Go-on girl," Ida said. "You and Black can both get out of here with your tale telling." "Aw Ida baby, come on and sit on daddy's lap. You know how much I love you. You are the only one for me." "If that is so Black, why don't you leave your wife? You've been sniffing around me for a lot of years. If you loved me…well, you know the rest." "Ida, now this ain't the time to talk about that. You know the woman I married all those years ago is a Catholic, and they don't believe in no divorce." I tell you what Black, if I had been married to your black ass and you didn't ever spend no time with me or my Grace, Catholic or no, I would have let you go a longtime ago." "Yea, but you ain't Catholic, and you ain't her. Baby, you know she's ugly too, and that's the other reason she won't let me go. Remember in the beginning when she used to come over and try to make me go home with her? Every time she looked at you, she saw what she wasn't. She knows she can't hold a candle to your adorable ass. So, I am here. Why do we have to go through this? I go to work, and I come home to you and Grace. Here, at this house," he said pointing to the floor. "I give you all of my money. I have given you my life, Woman! What else can I do Ida?" "Eat the damn gingerbread, Black," Ida replied. "That's what you can do. Just eat your gingerbread."

Annie could not figure why her husband Sonny did not want to be with her and their children. She kept a clean house, she kept her children clean and fed and she kept herself up as best she could. Although shy, she took an active role within the church and community. Everyone in Kendal Grove told her she was a good woman and a good mother. From Reverends Joe and James, Mrs. Carter, Mr. Howard and the other parishioners she received nothing but praise. She knew within herself she was a good person. A woman of God, who was raising her children in the church, the way they ought to be raised. Where did it seem to get her with her husband? Annie thought. She had a husband who cursed her, left her alone to take care of four children and gave her nearly enough money to live on. Then he was off for two or three months at a time. Maybe happiness with my husband was not for me, she thought. She felt overwhelmingly undesirable and pitiful. Even so, she was bent on praying for him to one day properly recognize and love his family. Eventually things would change, if she could hold out.

Usually on Saturday's Toby's was crowded, but on this particular night it was jammed packed. Sonny was surprised not to see Miss. Patricia with her man amongst the crowd. He wondered why she wanted to marry a Preacher, if she didn't want to act like a Preacher's wife. His sentiments were somehow she must derive some sort of pleasure of out of cheating on Kendal Grove's young preacher. Then he figured it was none of his business and turned his attention back to the crowd. There were so many people inside that he could roughly find a place to squeeze in at the bar. He scanned the room wondering where his "Sweetie Pie," as she like to be referred to lately, was. Grace was in the middle of a throng of men, all clamoring for attention. She was the prettiest thing at Toby's that night and every night. He downed his drink and decided to order another before rescuing his goodies. "Damn," he said to himself, thinking how difficult it was to get away from Annie this time? He knew she was trying her best to be a good mother, which she was. He had to give her that, and a good wife, but he wanted to be with his Sweeten Pie. Annie was nice and all that and she was beginning to fix herself up more. She has been looking right appealing lately, but she ain't Grace. Look at all those men around Grace, she is so pretty, so clean and fresh. Annie looks to tired and sad all of the time. Just as he began to move in the direction of Grace, he was halted by a strong grasp on his shoulder. "Not here and not tonight," he said to himself, "I'm not in the mood for a fight." Then he heard a familiar voice bellow from behind. "Is that how you treat an old friend, the one that got you that old crummy job you working on …BOY? Earl asked jokingly. As Sonny turned around, he said, "Boy, who you calling boy you old hunk of junk?" The two men embraced and patted each on the back. Sonny could not believe his eyes. Yes, it was Earl Case. The man who got him his job the man in no unspoken terms became his father. He opened his home to him and shared a world he may have never known existed. Fine things real fine things was the custom he remembered. Three square meals a day, fresh flowers throughout the house, carpeted floors, fresh linens and freshly pressed clothes, yard parties, plenty of food and a whole lot of good times. His wife, Estelle, who Sonny referred to as Momma Estelle, was a great housekeeper, cook and hostess. She was a dark woman, small in stature with a sturdy frame, kind and gentle with eyes that sparkled, dainty hands and a quick wit. The kind of woman with so much beauty in her soul it came out in everything she did. She was sought of like an angel, my angel, thought Sonny. "I remember now," he said to himself. "Annie. That's why I fell for her, she reminded me of my angel, Momma Estelle, soft, gentle and kind. That's why the preacher's family and everybody around Kendal Grove are so darn crazy about her. I had forgotten all about that." What's on your mind, Sonny?" Earl asked. "You look like your whole life just passed before your eyes." "It's just when I saw you Earl a lot of things that I had forgotten came back to me," Sonny replied. "Good things I hope, Boy?" "Yes, good things." "O.k., good stand here with an old man for a little while and let me buy you a drink. How is Annie doing, and those boys of yours?" "Aw, they're alright." "It's good to see you," said Earl. "It's good to see you too." "How is Momma Estelle?" "Estelle is fine. Damn, if Annie don't remind me of Estelle when she was young. The only thing that's different between them is that Annie is lighter, and Estelle has picked up some weight since she got older. But the two are so much alike. We said that to each other at your wedding but we never told you. I kept teasing Estelle for the longest time, are you sure you didn't run off and have some other man while I was on the road, because I swear that girl, Annie, could be your daughter?" Sonny didn't know how to react having a similar revelation. All he could do was smile. Earl went on to say, "I tell you boy, standing here and thinking back, I did some silly things in my day. But the Lord sure was good to me because he opened my eyes and allowed me to realize what I really had at home. I used to be a regular a few years ago, and had me a few women too. You had better watch yourself before you choke on that ice," Earl said stopping Sonny in the middle of a gulp. "Don't look so surprised, Sonny. I know you didn't know nothing about it. It's a whole lot of things you didn't know about. When I wasn't on the road, I used to wait until you and Estelle went off to sleep and I'd go off and have me a good time. Boy, you know how you are when your head hits the pillow. You are out for the night. Plus, I couldn't let you or no one else know my business. I didn't want to bring no harm to my family. I thank the Lord that I didn't, going through my trying to prove I was a man stage, when I was already a man. Nobody here was going to tell my business because they were doing the same dirt I was. So wasn't nobody telling on nobody for fear of their business getting out in the street. That was fifteen, no, twelve years ago. I had me a pretty, young girl too. Don't say nothing, cause I know what you thinking. But you are a man now, and you old enough to understand what I am saying to you. Let me take a look around to see if she is here tonight. Yep, there she is over in that corner, still pretty as she can be. Yea, still pretty as she was twelve years ago when I first saw her. She hasn't aged a bit. Her Momma ain't bad looking herself, and she has got to be around here somewhere," Earl said looking around the room. "Where is she, point her out to me?" said Sonny. "Look, over there sitting in the same old place she's been sitting since she first came in here at sixteen." Sonny could not believe his eyes, Earl was pointing in the direction of Grace. He couldn't mean Grace, but there was no other woman in full view or as pretty as Grace in the place, for that matter in the entire county of Parsons. "Earl went on to say, I don't think the girl knows about any other place except here and her home. I can't believe it, I haven't been in here for years, and she is still sitting in the same place. Guess she is still waiting for some dumb, old trucker. Thought I was someone important, I did. This woman walks over to me and says, "Hey Mister, my daughter is over there and this is her first night out. See, I don't want no little piss-ass punks messing around with my girl. I want her to start out with a real man and Mister it looks like you can play the part. She needs a real man to teach her about life. Come on over here and sit with us for a while." That was the line her Momma used on me and like a dumb old fish I took the bait. It took me a little time and several hundred dollars before I figured out I was only a small fish in Grace's pond. Those two are real big tricksters and have fools running around in circles playing their games. See, it goes like this: they wait for the truckers to come through town and pick one to be her main man. Believe me, there are just funning with him, because she has got more than a few on the side, and she is servicing every last one of them. Look at it like this, she ain't working nowhere, her Momma ain't working nowhere and look at their glad rags. I know that dress she's wearing cost $50 or more. And if you had ever gone to their place, she lives with her mother you see, you would think you were in a palace, and ain't neither one of them seen a day of labor of any kind. You know, I worked to make our place nice. Estelle and me, we've got it good. Compared to what those two have, it beats it all to hell." Sonny, dumbstruck, swallowed the last of his scotch in a gulp, and fixated on Grace's reflection from across the room in the mirror behind the bar. "Like I said that momma of hers, Ida, is a looker too. So is her momma's sister, Isabella. But they don't look as good as that girl of hers, Grace. Yea, three wicked women you want to avoid at all costs, Grace, Ida and Isabella. You alright, Boy, what are you doing here anyway? Are you going out on the road tonight?" "No, Daddy Earl, I'm not working tonight. As a matter of fact, I am going to thank you for this drink, and ask you to say hello to Momma Estelle. Give her a big old hug for me, and tell her I'll bring Annie and the boys to see her real soon. I am going home to my wife and children." Sonny shook Earl's hand and walked toward the door. "What you running off for?" asked Earl. "You ain't mad at me or nothing for sharing my business with you, are you?" "No, Daddy Earl, I am not mad at you, said Sonny. "I am eager to get home to my wife and children." "Well, alright then. Be careful out there. I am not long behind you." "You too," Sonny said turning toward the door. He tipped his hat to Ida and Black as they entered Toby's. Walked down the street, leaped into his truck and drove home to Kendal Grove to Annie and his boys.

Chapter Fifteen
PATRCIA'S OUTINGS

It had been almost five years with the Carter's day and night and Patricia remembered verbatim the last conversation between her and her grandmother. "You had to catch that boy didn't you?" Minnie asked Patricia. "There are so many places to go and things for you to do outside of this community. There are so many boys and young men in the world that would jump over backward to have you, but you had to set your eyes on someone who belongs to someone else. He doesn't love you and he won't. He was born to love one woman and one only. He will be a dutiful husband because he was bread that way. He will provide for you and be concerned about your wellbeing. You got what you think you wanted, but it will be the death of you. The saddest part about it is that you are a smart girl, a very smart girl, but too stupid to see what is wrong for you. Pattycake, go ahead have his child but don't marry him. You'll ruin both your lives." "Granny, don't marry him!" Patricia replied. "After all that preaching about finding the right man and making sure you're married before having any relations or bringing children into the world? What's wrong with you old woman? I thought you were dying." "I might be old, but I'm not too old to see that you still twist what people say to suit your wants. I love you girl, and yes, I am dying. I'm glad I'm not going to be around to watch you continue to make a mess out of your life and the good people around you. I wanted to try one last time to talk to you, and fix my breakfast. You know how I enjoy my coffee cake early in the morning. Everyone loves my coffee cake and it has been a joy for me to make. I tried several times to give you the recipe, but you didn't want it." "Why would I make it? You'll be here forever to make it yourself?" "No one is here forever, Pattycake." "Granny that old doctor doesn't know what he is talking about. Look at you up walking about and cooking. Ha, he only gave you a few days to live and that was last week. You've been healthy and strong as long as I can remember." "So you've been counting the days." "No, I haven't been counting the days at all. "If you had some money, I most likely would have been counting the days," Patricia said smiling. Minnie Haynes bowed her head partly in disgust and partly in shame, as she shook it slowly left then right. "It's truly a shame Lord that she can't, no she won't see it for what it is," Minnie sat talking the Lord. "Bless this poor child, please Lord, because I know I am about to leave this world." "Oh, no, here we go again," said Patricia. "Granny, where the hell are you going except back to bed? And the Lord, please what Lord?" "Don't blasphemy in my home, Patricia!" "All right, Granny, whatever you say. I have to go, anyway. One of the ladies from the church will check on you, if not Reverend Joe himself. He worries me asking about you, all of the time. Did you and he have some kind of fling?" "Goodbye, Pattycake, I hope one day you'll understand, and my living wasn't in vain. I really tried to do the best I could by you after your parents passing. You've definitely had a mind of your own since you came into this world. I'd say go right and you'd go left. I'd say don't and you would. I'd say stop and you'd go. I love you, though. You're a pretty thing. I hope your inwards catch up with your outwards." "Granny, what on earth are you talking about? Inwards catching up with outwards, I think my inwards are fine." "I know you do. That's the problem." "Granny, I would stay and chat with you a bit more, but I have to get going to see Mrs. Carter this morning to talk about the wedding." As Patricia got up from the table to leave, her grandmother grabbed her hand and kissed the back of it before rubbing it against her face. Granny is acting odd this morning, thought Patricia. She leaned over and kissed her grandmother on the forehead and pulled her hand away. Patricia didn't look back as she walked through the front door. Minnie ate her coffee cake and took her last sip of coffee in the quietness of their quaint little house.

The colors in her mind and the sound of her grandmother's voice were vivid. The part about her actually dying wasn't that bad because old people die, but the foretelling of a miserable life with Chaz Carter had come to pass and that was revolting. I had to run and leave my Granny to talk about the wedding with Mrs. Carter, she thought. "What wedding?" she said to herself, "it was just the Carter's and Ricky Stone. I didn't even have a maid of honor. They told me that because of my grandmother's death and funeral, and I was beginning to show that it wouldn't be appropriate for us to have a wedding or reception open to guests. I had to get married right in that dumb old living room with a homemade, child size wedding cake, and a stupid bouquet made out of flowers plucked out of Mrs. Carter's old worm infested garden. The only pure emotion she could summon up for the Carter's was hatred. As a matter of fact, she wasn't' sure if she ever really cared for any of them or their crowd, with the exception of Isaac and the late Lethea Howard, Lenora's parents. She never liked Chaz and merely wanted him so that Lenora couldn't have him, because she hated Lenora who had everything. Lenora was someone she hadn't thought about in ages. It no longer bothered Patricia that pictures of Lenora were beginning to appear all over the Carter's house again. I bet she'll never come back this way, after I had Chaz's baby, she thought. That was something she was sure that Lenora wanted from Chaz, a baby. "Come to think of it, the brat I had to have by Chaz Carter is just like them," she said to herself. "They can keep that boring, church going, crowd of theirs."

She loathed being in the presence of the Carters everyday, Sunday's were the worst. She had to attend the morning church services whether hung over or not. Whichever or whomever preached the sermon made no difference to her because they were all the same. This morning's speaker was Reverend James: "We find in the Old Testament in the Book of Exodus the Israelites seeking to bow down to something other than our God. They cast an idol, a golden calf, to worship instead of our God. I want you to think about what I said for a moment before I give you the title of this morning's sermon…The title of this morning's sermon is "Idols." What comes to mind when you hear the word "idol"? Do you only think of statues, monuments or pendants worn around the neck? On the contrary idols come in many forms, and are more familiar to you than you might think. Idols can be houses, land, money, your family, your children, yourself, love, want and even grief. Some of us can remember during the depression there was more than rain, hail, sleet and snow falling from the sky – men too were falling. Why? Because they had lost everything they had. They lost their idols. I see some of you looking around at each other laughing and saying, "We ain't never had nothing, no way." But that is wrong because everyone has something and some of you have idols too. Did you hear me when I said idols can be houses, land, money, your family, your children, yourself, love, want and even… grief. In other words if your entire life is wrapped in something you can't go without and you put it before God it's an idol. We made it through the depression and right now we are in this period of what's called "Recovery" but before Recovery, during Recovery and after Recovery you've learned it's not about what you got or what you've got left. It's about what you do with what you got! And what we've learned from our God is that if he takes it away from the righteous, he'll restore and give it back to you. Aw, he's a good and mighty God! Hallelujah! Some of us were the best dressed and we lost all of our clothes. Some of us had the best houses and we lost our homes. Some of us had money saved and have it no more. Some of us had strong backs, arms and legs that are not strong anymore, but we serve a mighty God who shall supply all our needs. The God who clothes us and gives us shelter will carry all of our burdens. Wahoo! His name is Jesus! He'll restore, He'll restore! What was lost will be found! Hallelujah! Hallelujah!" At the end of the sermon, Reverend James extended the invitation to discipleship and finally gave the benediction. Patricia stared at her watch in angst, thinking, only fifteen minutes left before I can have a drink, and leave for Toby's in Parsons. She had long ago abandoned the pretense of having an interest in the duties and pleasantries of fellowshipping with parishioners, before or after service as the wife of a clergy.

Toby's in Parsons was her sole respite. At Toby's she could sit back, watch the men one up themselves over her, dance, and leisurely inhale the aroma of the strong brown liquid before it eased down her throat. "No soda for me," she would say, "it makes my medicine too sweet. And with my daily headaches, I need all the medicine I can get." The affects of her "medicine" was significantly increasing her delusions and taking a toll on her life and everyone around her. More often than not under the influence of alcohol when leaving Toby's she would fall asleep at the wheel of Chaz's car on the back road to Kendal Grove. She was certain her sleeping in the car days were over, because she was positive that this was the night she would be sharing Martin Rhoads' bed in Parsons. Martin was a charming, tall, handsome, high yellow man with dark piercing eyes and jet black hair. Articulate, a neat dresser, and well built, he considered himself a gentleman and ladies man. In truth he was unstable, cruel and crooked to the bone. He carried a knife and used it readily on anyone who uncovered his schemes. In contradiction to his gentlemanly façade, his self professed hobby was "woman beating." Patricia fell for his good looks and gentlemanly charm with no reservations and enjoyed numerous romantic evenings with him at Toby's. The way he looked at her and held her when they danced sent her mind out of this world. He was a man, a real man and nothing like her mousy husband, she thought. Martin brought her drinks, flowers, and promised a multitude of gifts to follow. He even promised to cook for her one day. Although, brief their encounters, it couldn't be anything except real love she theorized. The invitation to spend the night with him was a longtime coming. Unreservedly she jumped at the prospect to spend the night at his apartment.

The apartment was spacious, nicely furnished and spotless. She sensed a woman's touch maybe from his mother, sister, or an aunt. It had two bedrooms, and was larger than her and Granny's house was. It was ideal, the right size for the two of them, she thought and envisioned in her mind. He sat a nice table and provided a good white wine and a good meal. Lamb chops with brazed carrots and green beans with shaved almonds. What a wonderful man he was to take the time to shave and add almonds to the green beans, she thought. Not only could he cook, but he knew good wine. She knew about wine because the Carter's had recently taken up serving wine at their countless dinners for ministerial dignitaries, family and friends. But the Carter's were far from her mind this night, because Martin made her feel sexy like the women in the Movies. A way in which she hadn't felt with Chaz since the first time she was close to him, the time she seduced him at that place, he and Lenora's place. Patricia couldn't wait to finish dinner so that Martin could hold her in his arms with no onlookers. She anticipated pure joy upon his touch as he came closer to her. What came next was something to ghastly to fully comprehend. Placing her hands in his, he squeezed as hard as he could, and abruptly pulled her to him. The impact of their bodies coming together knocked the wind out of Patricia, not to mention the agonizing pain felt in her hands. His rough and toothy kiss split her lips. The kiss was decisively different from his soft kisses at Toby's. Blood trickling down her chin, she wanted to yell out for him to stop, but she couldn't pull her mouth away from his, nor break free from his embrace. She caught her breath only when he snatched her away by the hair and hurled her headlong onto the sofa. Left breathless and dazed, she watched him tear at the buttons on his shirt. Shirtless, he unzipped his pants and came at her like a wild animal approaching its prey before devouring it. With one hand he yanked her bra and sweater up and over her breast. With the other hand he stuck it under her skirt and ripped off her panties. He then lifted her, turned her around, and flung her over the arm of the sofa. He hiked up her skirt to uncover her buttocks and drove his penis into her anus. Overcome with pain, worse than labor, she was about to scream. The words he spoke reeled her into a state of wordless shock. "If you scream bitch, I'll kill you," he snarled. Her feet were not touching the floor, and one of his hands was on her hip, and the other on her shoulder, pushing her down deeper and deeper into the sofa cushion. With no leverage she was unable to free herself from his grip. Helpless, she awaited his grunting and pounding to stop. His pounding stopped after he released a loud primeval groan and a tremendous pelvic thrust. He removed himself from her and said, “Stop acting like you didn’t like it. You know you like it, you bitch.” Stricken with fear, disbelief and excruciating pain, she didn’t know how to respond. The fact that she had been savagely and brutally battered and sexually assaulted was implausible. Again, Martin would get away with his heinousness, because of the shame associated with carnality outside the parameters of marriage. Patricia decided to relinquish what took place. It must be what other people do, she thought. And neither she nor her back woodsy husband were sophisticated enough to know. She recalled the first time she had sex with Ricky, it hurt too. So it must be the same type of thing. “If you don’t want to talk to me then don’t,” he said. “I really don’t give a damn. Now that you got what you wanted you can get your things and get the hell out.” “But Martin, I, I don’t,” she said with him interrupting. “You don’t what? “What, you didn’t know that I was going to give it to you like that? Shit, you lucky I gave you anything at all. You’re no different than the rest that come to Toby’s looking for some fun that you don’t get at home. I listened to you wine and cry and I gave you some of me to make you feel better. I can’t say it was a little of me because look at this thing.” Patricia, feeling nauseated and faint, couldn’t bring herself to look in the direction of his limp penis that he was waving in the air. “I need to wash up,” she said. “Well, go ahead.” “Where is the bathroom?” “Oh, you meant wash up here? Not here, you need to take yourself back to Kendal Grove to wash up,” he sneered. “Take your things,” he said, unfeeling, throwing her ripped panties, hat, coat and purse at her. Lethargic, Patricia collected her belongings from the floor and inched toward the door. When she passed him through the open door, she looked up into his eyes for some sort of compassion, or remorse for his actions. There was none. As she lowered her head, he said, “Meet me around the corner from Toby’s at the corner of 4th and Mead Street on Friday night at 8:00PM. And you’d better have that simple look off your face.” She nodded in agreement as the door shut and locked behind her.

Martin didn't have time for pleasantries after his deed was done with Patricia or any other woman he brought to the apartment. What Patricia and the people who frequented Toby's didn't know was that Martin was married. The apartment used for tonight's visit belonged to Martin's wife Susie, who sometime worked late into the evening. Separated from his wife, Martin had his own place at a small rooming house several blocks away. He couldn't take his conquests to his small, dingy and sparsely furnished room for his brand of entertainment. The cramped room didn't bother him since it wasn't much difference from the hovel he grew up in with his parents and six siblings. Better because he didn't have to share his one room with eight other people. He still had the key to Susie's and from time to time would drop by to leave a light on so that she wouldn't have to enter a dark apartment. He and his wife could no longer live together but they remained the best of friends. He had for Susie what he thought was the utmost consideration and respect unlike any he had before for another woman. For instance, he may bring a woman up to her place for a quick release from tension and the worries of this world, but he wouldn't kiss the women nor would he lie between their legs. That kind of loving was only for Susie, and heaven forbid, if he would ever sleep with another woman in her bed. That was the lowest of all the things he could do, because that was their marriage bed. Come to think of it, why did he refer to those things, those low life heifers as women? Most of them were sluts and whores running around on their husbands, who didn't appreciate what they had at home. None were like his Susie, a dark skinned, plump and soft woman who was good to look at. She was smart, kind, a good cook, a good housekeeper and a successful business woman. She was a self-made Negro woman who owned two beauty shops. A good woman, a good Christian woman who no one found fault in. Unbeknown to Martin she was considered to have one fault, her marrying and continuing a relationship with him. He was trash and everyone knew it, except Martin and Susie.

It was a cold, windy and snowy Friday night and Martin was over two hours late. Patricia was soaked to the bone from the heavy snow fall. She made up her mind to head back to Kendal Grove for a hot meal and a hot bath, when a car pulled up to the curb causing a wave of water to splash her from head to toe. After catching her breath and wiping the dirty street water from her face, she proceeded to tell the unknown driver how inconsiderate they were for splashing her. What she didn't know was that it was Martin behind the wheel and she was splashed for his amusement. He could tell by her expression that her response to his little joke was not appreciated at all. He swiftly exited his car, grabbed her by the throat and hurled her against the brick wall of Mead Bank and Trust. He held her throat so tightly that she could not breathe nor speak. Face-to-face, with his body pressed to hers, he asked her, "What you got to say now, bitch?" He then kissed her softly on the lips, and punched her in the mid section. Crumpled to the pavement, he landed a blow to the right side of her face before landing another to the left side of her face. Practically unconscious he grabbed her by her coat collar and pulled her to her feet, only to throw her back down to the pavement. He started toward her again, stopped, and said, "Aw the hell with you," returned to his car and drove away. Martin lost interest in his assault because she wasn't participating to his liking. There wasn't any screaming or cussing, nor was she fighting back. He found no real pleasure in beating a woman who wouldn't fight back. It was to Patricia's advantage that she had all bark and no bite. She never had to fight or defend herself physically, so she didn't know how. It was with her nasty tongue her battles were fought, bringing many to deep despair and rendered helpless. Her pearl encrusted hairpin that she wore on special occasions, as was all of her manicured and polished fingernails were broken. Most of her hair was loosely hanging down over her shoulder, while the rest was still pinned in place with the few hairpins that remained. Her face was swollen, badly bruised and bleeding. She was also cold and wet, but her greatest concern was finding her purse, which was becoming more difficult to clearly see due to her left eye swelling shut. On her hands and knees she gathered her composure and located her small black clutch purse leaning against the brick wall of the bank, as if she intentionally put it there. With purse in hand, she used her free hand to brace herself, as she attempted to stand. She wasn't sure if her shoes were loose courtesy of Martin, or if her legs were wobbling due to his blows to her face. Nonetheless, she was about to fall, when the strangest thing happened, all of a sudden there was a man there to support her. Her first reaction was apprehension and she tried to recoil. She didn't have enough energy to do very much of anything except go where she was led. "Let me help you," he said. "It's alright. I'll help you, lean on me." That's all she remembered until she awoke on a dark red sofa, under a cream colored coverlet, surrounded by what looked like a dozen pillows. She could see that the abrasions on her hands and knees were attended too, but she wanted to see her face. More importantly where was she? And who was the sleeping man sitting in the brown wing back chair across from her? She awoke him when she began to maneuver her way out of the manmade cocoon. "Wait a second there now, take your time," he said. "The time," she replied, "what time is it?" "It is 4:30AM, Saturday morning," he said pointing to the clock over the fireplace. "Do you remember what happened to you?" "Of course I do," she shot back. "He's crazy, and I was crazy to think he liked me." "I am not going to get into that. Are you hungry? Would you like a drink, or would you like to use the bathroom?" "Yes. I would to everything you asked. But no liquor, I'll take soda water with ice." It wasn't until she tossed the coverlet off that she realized she wasn't wearing anything but a man's undershirt and socks. "Where are my clothes?!" She demanded massaging her aching head with both hands at her temples, trying to ease the pain. "Your coat, dress and under garments are all hanging in the kitchen near the stove to dry. Your shoes are in there too, and your handbag is on the end of the table next to where you are sitting. The bathroom is down the hall to your left. Holler if you need me, I'll be in the kitchen fixing your tray. Oh, by-the-way, my name is Carl." Thank God he's not crazy like Martin, she thought carefully walking to the bathroom. She decided to relieve herself before peering into the mirror to access the damage done to her face. "Damn it!" Patricia exclaimed when she saw her reflections. “Damn it to hell!” she said when she touched her swollen and blackened eye and her swollen and split lips. “I can’t believe this! Will you take a look at my flawless face? I look like I have the mumps, or I am an ugly field hand. I might as well be a damn Picker looking this way!” Her reaction to her reflection and comments were unlike any woman’s he had ever heard before. He wanted to ask her what a “Picker” was but didn’t. He was accustomed to witnessing similar incidents frequenting juke joints and after hour clubs. The battered women would pour out their hearts and lament over their lover’s destructive behavior. They would make excuse after excuse for his shortfalls and tout his favor. She seemingly had no concern what-so-ever about the actions or whereabouts of her lover Martin. She had no idea that Carl knew what she looked like before the beating. They talked non-stop for the next five hours about famous personalities, current events and their mutual interests. Still no mention of Martin, or wait a second, her name, he thought. “What is your name?” he asked, cutting her off in the middle of a sentence. “Patricia, Patricia Wynn,” she answered. “Where are you from?” “Not far from here,” she answered. “Are you married?” “Yes.” “Do you love your husband?” “No,” she answered. “Then why don’t you divorce him?” “That would be difficult.” “Why?” “Let’s say we’ll discuss it another time.” Her responses intensified his interest in her more. “Are you ready to go home, or do you have to make a call to let anyone know where you are?” “I would like to make a telephone call, but I don’t want to go home until the swelling goes down in my face.” “The telephone is down the hall. I wouldn’t mind putting you up for a week or so, if you don’t mind sharing my place? I’ll take the sofa and you can take my bed.” Patricia had no hesitation, whatsoever, accepting his offer to stay. “Hell yea!” She said to herself, “Anything, well almost anything, is better than going back to the Carters’. And this man is a good looking man too, she thought. Good solid build, dark skinned, wavy hair, bright eyes and the prettiest smile she’d ever seen on a man. He’s been places and done things and he’s smart. He’s nothing like her boring limp penis husband.

Patricia hastily donned her dress and dashed to the hall telephone shared by all of the occupants of the two story apartment building. "Yes, Mrs. Carter, I'm fine," she whispered into the mouthpiece of the telephone. "I've decided to stay over at my girl friends house for awhile. Her mother hasn't been feeling well, and Carly, my girlfriend, needs a helping hand." "Patricia that's very kind and thoughtful of you," she heard Bertha say through the receiver. "How long did you say you'd be there?" Bertha asked. "Oh, I'll stay for a week or so." "Where are you? Is there a telephone number where we can reach you?" "Sorry, Mrs. Carter there are others waiting to use the telephone. I'll call you at the end of the week. Ya'll take care." Patricia hung up the telephone to avoid further questions from Bertha, and having to make up lies to tell her in response to her questions. She took a deep breath and exhaled before reentering Carl's apartment. This is going to work out fine, she could feel it. The life she'd always wanted was finally at her fingertips.

Carl Houston was something to look at. Handsome on the same lines as Martin, yet there was an air of distinction and splendor about him. Never one who had to chase women, he was fine and women clamored to him. Athletically built, he was pleasing to the eye fully dressed or undressed. The myth was found real when it came to the size of his big hands and big feet; his member had both length and girth. The first time he fully undressed and exposed his exquisite form to Patricia she found it hard to withstand the temptation to lick him from the soles of his feet to the crown of his head. She wanted to give him all that she could.

Overnight it seemed Carl fell in love with Patricia. Patricia on the other hand was madly in love with Carl being in love with her. There were no words for Patricia to describe their passionate, slow and easy love making. During the first year of their relationship he took his time to know and enjoy every inch of her supple and curvaceous body. He was in love and couldn't get enough of her while she couldn't get enough of having sex with him. She no longer needed the three or four cocktails after dinner for stimulation, like she did with Chaz, because Carl supplied all the stimulation needed to produce her multiple orgasms. His muscular and flawless body gave way to her desire to admire, prod and probe an excellent male specimen. His lingering kisses and gentle touch reminded her of apple blossom petals softly falling on her, caressing her neck, shoulders, arms, breast, stomach and legs which made her shiver at his touch. The satisfying aroma of their bodies flowing through the air saturated her senses and prompted her natural instincts to jostle her hips in accordance with his rhythmic momentum as he made his way inside her before succumbing to a paralleled end. He made her feel so good. And the gifts of candy, flowers and shopping money he afforded were non stop. There was nothing she wanted that he didn't provide her when she visited. Shopping at Carl's expense was how she met the flamboyant Dwight Benton over a jewelry counter at Parson's Department Store. "Is it anything you are looking for in particular, Miss?" Dwight asked. "Why yes," Patricia answered. "I would like to replace my pearl hair comb. As you can see it has been broken? You have on your overcoat. It was very nice of you to stop before you left for the day to inquire about me." "This is not my place of employment. I wanted to inquire about you," he said undressing her with his eye. "Because girl, you look good enough to eat." "Yes, I do," she said smiling. "Then why don't you let me?" "I don't know your name, Sir," she said not allowing him to finish his sentence. You shouldn't speak to me in that manner." "My name is, Dwight." "What, no last name?" "Not until I know your first and last name." "It looks like I won't know your last name then," she said turning her attention back to the display case. "Maybe not today, but I'll see you around, and I'll get it," he said slipping his personal card on top of the display case in front of her. "That is your name, and anything else I want," he said learning over her shoulder. Patricia shivered with curiosity only to turn around to find he was gone. Nothing had tantalized her in that way since her first meetings with Martin. Dwight intrigued her and she wanted to learn more about him. Patricia liked Carl whole heartedly. He was definitely a very good means to end her terrible life with the Carters. In truth, she knew that she could only be true to her one true love, and that was none other than herself. She couldn't wait to give Dwight a ring on her next visit to Parsons.

Chapter Sixteen
MARIANNE'S DECISION

It was the fault of a careless driver that shortened her husband's life on a rainy Thursday evening. The traffic light was red, but it didn't matter due to her unwillingness to stop, even if someone was crossing the street. She was late for her weekly bridge club meeting and that was more important than stopping for a traffic signal. Mrs. Tillie Beeker, the sister-in-law of the Mayor, had no intentions on stopping knowing she hit something. What prompted her to stop was one of her headlamps ceased to work making it challenging to navigate the road. In her rearview mirror she noticed a crowd had gathered around whatever she hit, so she might as well turn the car around to take a quick look. A bloody Negro, wearing a very nice and expensive raincoat, lay crumpled next to the sidewalk. His shoe, at least the one shoe he was wearing, was very nice and expensive too. She than noticed the blood oozing from a large crack in the middle of his forehead and his eyes, staring straight into the rain. She'd never seen anyone look into the rain without blinking before. "Didn't he hear me honk my horn?" She said to the crowd. "Can you believe the nerve of some Negro people? He shouldn't have been crossing the street when I was coming through. My husband is the brother of the Mayor, and he say's, "Negro's are stupid when it comes to things like reading and obeying the law." When the officer arrived at the site of the accident Tillie casually waved her right hand and said, "Officer, I am Tillie Beeker, the sister-in-law of the Mayor. Take care of this will you." In death, Highlife was charged with Jay Walking, and the sister-in-law of the Mayor was cleared of any wrong doing.

"Dr. Wendell Heights is no longer with us because he has gone on to a better place," said the Minister at the cemetery. "Yet his memories will remain with us forever." Marianne the professor's devoted wife;

the consummate partner was without Highlife for the first time in her life. Isaac interlocking his left arm with her right arm, holding her hand and James interlocking his right arm with her left arm, with Bertha close behind, escorted her back to the long black funeral car. She was grateful for the presence of her beloved friends, but all she could do was cry. Distraught she wanted to break free, grab her head and yell so loud that it could be heard all the way to the Mayor's house. The Dean of the college walked over to the car as Marianne, Bertha, James and Isaac settled inside. He spoke to Marianne in a hush tone saying, "My dear Marianne, we are so sorry for your loss. I want you to know that there is no real rush, but we'd like to ready the house you're in for the new Professor. He'll be arriving in two weeks." Taking her gloved hand into his, he said, "Me and the Mrs. won't be able to attend the repast, but remember we deeply feel your loss. It was nice meeting all of you." He closed the car door and back away from the car as it pulled off exiting the cemetery. No words transpired between the old friends. They were insulted and the memory of Highlife had been insulted. The pain they felt was beyond measure.

Marianne had no choice except to move out of their palatial campus home into a tiny apartment on the other side of town. This is how the life of a brave and dedicated man ends. What was all of it for? The years of working his way through school, studying and teaching? All of his note books, papers, awards and citations fit into two crates that go into storage. She chuckled at the thought of what Highlife might think after all of the wooden boxes he built working his way through college. Now what was he, my great Professor of Philosophy, quoted for saying, "The old produces the new and nothing is fact except you are born and you die." She handled her grief by concluding all of their business affairs and clearing Highlife's schedule. He had four speaking engagements left in the year and she spoke at each one in his stead. Having no children or relatives to encourage or support her efforts the college Chaplin and her Kendal Grove friends were her staunch supporters.

Regularly and empathetically Marianne and Isaac corresponded and spoke on the telephone. She needed him and he needed her. When Isaac arrived to escort her back to Kendal Grove for a visit it was decided she would be going back for good. Impressed by her strength and courage his devoted friendship turned into love. They were married just outside a year of Highlife's prang in a private ceremony by the college Chaplin. The Chaplin's wife and son witnessed their nuptials.

The union of Isaac and Marianne was blissful and mutually rewarding. Isaac was a loving and attentive husband, who assured both her needs and wants. Marianne was more than a companion she was a loving, insightful and intelligent woman worthy of full partnership. She had good business sense and he marveled at her talents and abilities in retailing. The many things they had in common further fueled the passion in their relationship. Unlike her marriage to Highlife where her daily functions were catered to satisfying his needs and pursuits, her wants and needs were not encouraged or fulfilled. Isaac shared everything with her and acted on her insightful suggestions to increase store revenue. She suggested rearranging the general store for more accessibility to items to better suit the needs of the customer, and the start-up of a new entity. "The ladies have to practically climb over crates, buckets and other merchandise to get back to a little corner to look at or try a dress," she said. "Or order a dress from a catalog and have to wait for weeks on end to receive it. No, Isaac that won't do. I want a separate store where woman can buy garments and there can be a section for men too. Picture it, hats, gloves, sweaters, dresses, coats, braziers, and I mean good quality stuff. And for the men suits, ties, shirts, socks, jackets, slacks and overcoats. We have the space if the largest storage area is cleared painted and carpeted."

The largest storage area for the general store was converted into a fine clothing store, with a separate entrance, for the men and woman of Kendal Grove. The floor was carpeted in dark green and the walls were painted walnut brown. There was a cash register counter and one fitting room with surround mirrors in each department. The shoes were stocked behind the counters and the shoe samples were dispersed throughout the departments on display as were manikins arrayed in the latest fashions for sale. It also had a small tailoring shop. Both male clerks and both female clerks had tailoring skills. Each purchase was wrapped in tissue paper before placement in a paper bag or box with Howard's Apparel embossed on it. Dottie who remained in the household as part of the family was in on the enterprise as well. She made and supplied ladies hats, scarves, handkerchiefs, aprons, and doilies, for a decent profit. Marianne's fashionable sense of style and incredible way with people made Howard's Apparel a lucrative success.

Chapter Seventeen
THE PLAN

"Guess who I talked to the other day," Bully asked his son as they were putting the final touches on the new church shutters. "Who Daddy?" asked Carl. "Joe Carter. They are holding their annual picnic and wanted to make sure we're coming, since we haven't been in years. Wouldn't you know your Momma has already committed that weekend to speak at the Annual Women's Conference? Just the same, I told him I would come and you should go with me Carl. I know they all would be glad to see you, especially Chaz. You haven't seen your old chum for more than eight years." "That's right Daddy, how time really fly's. I think that is a good idea, I really want to go. Thanks for mentioning it to me." "You know what, son?" "What?" "At first I thought green wouldn't do this old church no justice. Now that I get a good look at it, it works. The green against the white kind of grows on you. Praise God, it really looks nice. We are still the painting duo," said Bully. He was very pleased to have his son Carl again working at his side. It had been many years since they worked together to complete a project. At one time Carl was considered to be his shadow when it came to working with his hands. You could count on the Houston's for carpentry, painting, and paving and when it came to such tasks as shoveling snow, they even did that together.

The truth of the matter was that Bully was taking full advantage of his son's renewed interest in doing things together once more. He loathed the way Patricia lied, cheated and trampled the hearts of those he loved. Yet the affections she bestowed on his son were making a real man out of him. He shook his head at the thought of her and his son together. The Lord truly works in ways unbeknown to man. He prayed, "Hear my prayer, oh most merciful Lord, please guide me to do what I know has to be done with my son. Please help me continue to lift and encourage him. I know his heart will be broken but I know that you are a God that mends the broken hearted. Thank you, precious Father for allowing us to have our son back. In the precious name of Jesus I pray, Amen." "What are you over there mumbling about, Daddy?" "The usual Carl, I am just talking to the Lord."

Carl was enjoying spending time with his folks. He was realizing the importance of family. Patricia probably would not accept his proposal, if she knew that his relationship with his parents had been strained over the years, at no fault of theirs. Since she was in such a bad situation, as she liked to refer to her marriage, he would provide a stable home for her to enjoy for the rest of their lives. After they settled then maybe they could have a few kids. With her looks their children would be beautiful. She would be a great mother, he thought. "Daddy, when is the picnic?" Carl asked. "It's next Saturday, I'll be leaving her around 1:00PM." Carl looked disappointed because he hoped to spend most of each Saturday with Patricia as he regularly did. "What's wrong, you can make it can't you? "Yes, I can make it. That's not a problem. I was thinking I might want to ask someone to go with us." "And who would that be?" "Don't worry, Daddy, she is really a good person. I just remembered, she can't go anyway because she'll be out of town this coming weekend."

"Come on, Carl. Let's get these things put away before dark." Bully changed the subject to avoid his true thoughts and feelings coming to light. "I cannot believe she has my son, Mr. Lover Boy, so fooled," he said to himself. She will be out of town, what a laugh, he thought to himself. Bully shook his head with disgust. That woman is every bit of a jezebel. "Lord, I know you reap what you sow," Bully prayed, "please have mercy, and help my son, hear your servant's prayers. Lord, hear my prayer." "I think, I'll go on home, Daddy," Carl said as he slid into his new Packard. "Tell Momma, I'll talk to her later." "Alright son, see you Saturday afternoon."

Carl loved his new car. He felt overjoyed and began talking to himself and than to the Lord. "I have got it now!" Carl said to himself. "I have got everything I have ever wanted in this life. I have my health, my parents, a good job, this brand new car and a beautiful woman who loves me, who also happens to look great in my car." "It has been a longtime since I have spoken to you, Lord. I mean it looked to me as if all the fun things to do in life were wrong. So I turned my back on trying to please you and I only worried about pleasing myself. I drank some. No, let me tell the truth, I got pissy drunk many times. I hustled to turn a buck, and I womanized. From what I've been told, I broke a lot of hearts. But during all that I must have done something right because I am one happy man. I have got everything! Lord, I will propose to her next week. I know she isn't divorced yet, and you don't look favorable on the life we have been leading. You know my heart and you know I want to be an honorable man. She is mistreated and her life is miserable with that old drunken husband of hers'. Thank you Lord for sending Patricia to me, because she has really changed the way I see and do things. Thank you, Lord for not forsaking me, and allowing me the opportunity to speak to you again. I know you hear my prayer. Please, show me what to do, make me a good man and a faithful husband for a good and faithful woman, Amen. Oh yea, in the name of Jesus Christ my Lord and Savior I pray, Amen." How long had it been since he uttered those words? It felt reassuring to know that the Lord God was with him. He knew the Lord heard his prayer and it would be answered. On Sunday I will surprise daddy and mother by taking my place again beside mother in church, he thought, and soon, Patricia will be joining me on the pastor's family pew.

Chapter Eighteen
THE ANNUAL PICNIC

"Patricia darling, I need you to peel those potatoes for the potato salad a little faster," Bertha said. Patricia cut her eyes at Bertha and took a deep sigh. She could care less about all the fuss for the annual family picnic or anything else the Carter's did. The only reason she volunteered to peel the boiled potatoes was that it provided something for her to do with her hands. Otherwise, she was sure to be in a drunken stupor. Unable to get away from her so called "family obligation" to be with Carl for the weekend, all she wanted to do was drink. A few drinks now and then were the only thing that kept her sanity around the Carters. These people and their-think-they-are-grand life drives me crazy, she thought. "They can keep that little brat of Chaz's that they constantly make over," she said to herself peeling potatoes. "It will be me and my man, Mr. and Mrs. Carl Houston. I'll make him so happy he won't think about me having children. I don't want to have anymore anyway. I don't and didn't want the one I've got. If it wasn't for Lenora having everything I wouldn't be in this situation. Damn! I can't wait to get away from here." "Patricia, would you bring over to the sink the potatoes you've finished peeling?" Bertha asked. It was then Patricia picked up on the conversation that Bertha was having with the other women in the kitchen. "You mean to tell me that Uncle Joe was in love with another woman besides, Aunt Georgia?" Kitty asked. "Yes, Kitty that's right." The other women all much older than Patricia and Kitty nodded in agreement. "I thought they were a perfect couple like you and Uncle James and your friends Mr. Isaac and Miss. Lethea, who passed on, and now with his new wife, Miss. Marianne? You all grew up together and became great loving couples." "Yes. That's right, but Daddy Joe and Miss. Savanna grew up together, too. Although, I think he is between seven or eight years older than she is." "Who is Miss. Savanna?" Kitty asked. "I don't think I've ever heard of her before." "Yes, you have. You have heard of her and you have seen her many times, at least those times when you came to visit us. You've spent many hours in the back of her establishment watching baseball games." The conversation caught Patricia off guard. Never before this day had she remembered a time when she was interested in anything Bertha had to say. Who on earth was this Miss. Savanna? She thought. Patricia or Kitty hadn't a clue as to what Bertha was talking about. Kitty had visited Kendal Grove for Camp Meetings and for family gatherings all of her life, but there was no memory of meeting anyone by the name, Savanna. "Was her Aunt losing her mind as she was growing older?" Kitty asked herself. "Aunt Bertha, I don't mean to sound rude, but the only place to watch baseball games is at Sassy's diamond behind her beer garden. You know, the place where people go to dance." "They drink there too, Kitty, don't they?" "Yes Mam." I didn't want to mention that." "Like I said, Kitty you have watched baseball games behind her establishment." "You mean, Miss. Sassy's real name is Savanna, and Uncle Joe used to be in love with her?" "Yes, I do." "What?" Kitty said exactly what Patricia was thinking. If anyone had looked her way they would have noticed her chin dropping inches above the floor. At least that's how she felt when she heard the jaw dropping piece of news. "Mr. Joe and Miss. Sassy were in love with each other long ago?" Patricia said to herself. "No. Miss. Sassy was too full of life and vigor for him." "What happened?" Kitty asked. "Why didn't they get together?" "Circumstances, I guess," said Bertha. "What circumstances?" "People, things," Bertha said holding up the pie pan in her left hand and trimming the excess crust from the edges of it. "From what I understand, Joe and Savanna were very much in love," added Cousin Molly stirring the punch. "His mother, my Aunt Flora, wouldn't have it because she had her eye set on someone else for Joe. In addition, Savanna lost her mother, and shortly thereafter her broken hearted father went to pieces and lost his mind. He was a mean man before his wife died, and afterward he became worse.

She had to leave home. Having no kin, no one to take her in and no money she had no place to go. That's when old Smokey took her in. He ran this little shack, where people would go to gamble and drink. He gave her a room on the second floor of the shack to call home, and he put her to work as a waitress. She was always pretty and full of life, and when she was young, she was a killer diller. Men started coming in just to look at her. They spent so much time at Smoky's that their wives and girlfriends started coming with them. It was really no need for the women to be jealous because Savanna never paid no mind to any of their advances. She had a way of making a man pant after her, turn him down and then switch away. That's why Smoky called her "Sassy" and the name stuck. That old shack went from what it was to what it is today. Although, she was like a daughter to him, people didn't like a young girl living with a man who wasn't her kin." "No one would take her in when her father threw her out, and when somebody did they talked about it," said Kitty. "That's the way it is Kitty with some people, including those we love, like my grandmother and James' grandmother," Bertha replied. "Grandmother Carter wasn't going to let her son marry anyone who worked about gambling and drinking people." "Was this before Uncle Joe became a preacher," asked Kitty? "It sure was," said Molly. These things took place before he became a preacher. We came to realize that she never liked Savanna, and surely didn't want her as a daughter-in-law." "So, old Joe had some fire in his pants," said Patricia. "What are you saying Patricia?" Bertha asked. "All I am saying is that if Sassy was ever interested in Reverend Joe, he must have had some real fire in his britches," Patricia said. "I can't imagine her being interested in no diaper wearing, Momma's boy. Than on the other hand, I guess he really is a diaper wearing Momma's boy, because he didn't marry her, did he?" Kitty began to laugh and than decided to clear her throat instead, as not to disrespect her Aunt Bertha. "Patricia, whether or not they got married is not the issue. We were discussing relationships," said Bertha. "So was I," replied Patricia. "No matter what I say, it's wrong," she mumbled. Bertha continued, "I think this is a good time to curtail this discussion. Patricia, please finish peeling those potatoes. We have other chores to do before our guest arrive."

As the guest began to arrive, Patricia couldn't help wishing it would rain and all the guests leave for their own homes. She thought it would be funny to see a lightening bolt strike Victoria. She made the best fried chicken in Kendal Grove but the round, mean and nasty gossip could use a lightening bolt right to the mouth. She smiled, envisioning the imaginary rainstorm, and the guests running to and fro in chaos, and Victoria's lips sealed together by a lightening strike. It was then she heard her name called, and snapped back, "What is it Chaz?" Patricia hated the sound of his voice, particularly when he called her name. "Mother is looking for you to help with the finishing touches around the serving area," he said. "All of these people around here, and she is looking for me?" Patricia said unwilling to help. "I know that some of them would be more than willing to help her. Why doesn't she call on her sainted few? Where is Dottie, Marianne, Madeline or Annie? Why doesn't she ask them to help her instead of worrying me?" "Patricia these are our guests, this is our home, and it is our honor to serve them." "Oh no, my dear Chaz it's an honor to be served, and that you obviously can't do in more ways than one." She grabbed his arm to bring him closer to her and whispered into his ear, "Do you hear me young Preacher-man, you can't serve me," before briskly sashaying away. She had already had enough of this day and she wanted it over.

Chaz ignored the sordid remark from Patricia, like he did her others, and went about his way greeting their guests. He was accustomed to her offensive and absurd remarks and there wasn't much she could say or do to offend him anymore. He had done everything he could to make her happy. He prayed for years without ceasing for a blessed marriage. His continuous prayers had become more directed to his ministry, the wellbeing of his son, his parents and for those who could not help themselves. He figured Patricia fell within the last category because she insisted on making her own decisions no matter how destructive, no matter who was harmed. Patricia must have thought the hatred she directed at him over the years must be killing him. Little did she know that the hatred he had for himself, for lying with her in the first place, registered degrees above her hatred for him. Without the time taken out of his day for his personal one-on-one time with God he knew that he would all but perish. He still tormented himself for that one moment of fleshly desire. Before that time he knew nothing of failing to temptation. "Why and how could he have failed himself and Lenora? Chaz asked himself. He missed Lenora terribly. He had not seen her in over five years and hadn't written her once since the "incident." The "incident," he referred to the time when he and Patricia laid together and conceived their son. They laid together in their place, he and Lenora's place. The punishment of being in an unmanageable marriage with Patricia appeared justifiable because he had defiled everything he and Lenora stood for. How long would this punishment last because at times it was unbearable. It was unthinkable for Chaz to hate anyone but himself, but if he could, he was sure he would hate Patricia. The cruelty to Chaz and his parents from her was more tolerable. However, the cruelty to their son was appalling. She acted like a miserable being filled with hatred. He was sure that if she took the hatred and turned it into love and did good works for the Holy Father, it would truly be a blessing. He took joy in hoping that was the Lord's plan. He also wondered if Lenora would ever forgive him for betraying her, or ever trust him again. "What a terrible man she must think I am, I truly miss her," he said to himself. "Our annual picnic was one of the events she looked most forward too."

Ice tea and more ice tea, Patricia thought, will they ever get enough? "I've been washing glasses since two o'clock this afternoon," she said to herself. "I tried to get my dear mother-in-law to buy the new paper kind, but no, she wouldn't hear of it. "It would insult my guest to have them drink from cheap paper cups," she said. Why am I complaining? I get to stay inside, all by myself, and I don't have to fake playing the happy wife, mother or daughter-in-law. I'll stay inside, wash these glasses and think about my Big Daddy, Carl. I wish Chaz was half the man that Carl is. Mr. Goody-goody, oh how I love the Lord, wouldn't know a real man like Carl. Does he think of me like I think of him? I know he is going to ask me to marry him soon. And as soon as he does ask me to marry him, I am gone! I will move in with him, and he will pay for my divorce. I will never have to look at these boring people again as long as I live. No more little brat, no more old people, and no more got-to-go-to-church every damn day folks. The lay back and relax life is for me and my man. I'm going to be riding in his brand new car with my hair blowing in the wind. I can't wait to march into Toby's with our matching wedding bands. Get back, yea, I got him and he is all mine ladies. And you, Martin Rhoads, look what your beating got me, more man than you'll ever be."

Carl had not taken a ride with his father for years. "Dad, why are you so quiet over there?" Carl asked. "When I was a little boy and we took a ride to Kendal Grove you used to talk me and Momma's ears off." "That's why I am not saying anything," answered Bully. "I must have said all of what I had to say." "Daddy, you never can say enough." They laughed. Bully wasn't talking because he was nervous. "What will he do when he sees her Lord?" Bully asked silently. "What will I say? Will he hate me?" The questions revolved in his mind. "Bless my son Lord. Please hold his heart, tongue and body in your hands. Bless him Lord." "What did you say, Dad?" "Didn't know I said anything boy, I'm talking to the Lord." "Look Dad, there it is," Carl said pointing to the Carter's home. "Woo, look at all the people. I had forgotten how many come out to this thing." "They sure do. You'll probably see people that you wouldn't think would be here." "I can surely believe that. There is an open space, park over there, Dad. Come on Dad, I can't wait to see Chaz, Aunt Bertha, Uncle James and Reverend Joe." Carl's enthusiasm to visit with their oldest friends was remarkable. Unfortunately, Bully knew that the enthusiasm of his son would soon turn to sorrow. "Look Dad, there's Reverend Joe." When Joe saw Carl, he arose from his game of checkers and began half running and half walking towards him. "Look at you boy, look at you," said Joe. The old man and young man embraced. "I am so glad to see you, Carl." "Is that all you see?" Bully asked. "I ain't talking to you, I'm busy," said Joe. They laughed. "I guess I'd better go on home then." "Not until you eat, Bully. If Bertha found out you were here and didn't eat…that would be the end of me. You trying to get me hurt?! Come on here and let's find Chaz and Bertha." Reverend Joe led his best friend and Godson toward the house. "Well, for the lands sake," said Bertha spying Bully and Carl out of the other guests coming in her direction. "You had better give me a big old hug, and kiss me, boy. My, you look good, how is life treating you, Carl?" "I am fine, thank you, Aunt Bertha." "What is this, Bertha?" asked Bully. "Is he all you see, did you forget all about me?" "What are you talking about, Uncle Bully?" Bertha asked. "Your old father-in-law acted like he didn't see me. And look at you kissing all over that boy of mine. You haven't given me a kiss since the day me and Joe married you off." "You two had to marry me off, did ya?" "Wasn't nobody else going to marry you or that lanky husband of yours. So we had to marry you off to each other." "Lanky?" said James as he came near their dear friends. "I have you know that I am considered tall, dark, trim and extremely handsome." "I guess people don't tell you the truth about your skinny, long-legged self out of respect for your father and all," said Bully. "People have respect for those real, real old folks and such." "Old, old, now Bully you know when God said, "Let there be light," you were there to light the lanterns," said Joe. They burst into uncontrollable laughter including those standing close by. "I am so sorry that Rachel had to attend the Woman's Conference, and couldn't be here with us today, Bertha," said Bully. "Where is Chaz?" Carl asked. "He is around somewhere," said Bertha. "Ya'll go on over there and fix yourselves a plate. I'm sure you'll find one another. We couldn't keep you two apart for two seconds, when we used to visit each other."

Carl sat down at a picnic table with his father and several other men from Kendal Grove to eat his scrumptious meal. Some he remembered from his frequent visits as a child. Others he didn't remember, but he enjoyed their company just the same. "Is that you,

Carl Houston," said Chaz. Carl arose from the table and said, "Yea man, it's me." The two young men hugged, stood back and shook each other. "Man, I haven't seen you for years," said Chaz. "I thought you had fallen off the edge of the earth." "Naw man, I am fine, I am doing great," said Carl. Joey came running calling out to his father, "Daddy! Daddy! Daddy!" Picking up is son Chaz asked, "Are you having a good time, Joey?" Joey shook his head up and down to indicate yes. Chaz than introduced his son to Mr. Carl Houston, his childhood friend. Carl shook Joey's little hand and said, "Young Sir, I am truly glad to meet you." "Thank you," Joey replied. "I am glad to meet you, too." Chaz put his son down, and before he could pat him on the top of his head, he darted off to play with the other little boys at the picnic. "Gosh Chaz," said Carl. "That little big eyed, curly head boy looks like you. He is a handsome little man and his curls are as big as my thumb. No offense man, but do you realize his head is shaped like your Granddaddy's?" "Why do you think we call him, Joey? When he was born he came out looking like my Grandfather. He didn't start looking like me until he was two years old." The two men laughed and continued their conversation catching up on each others lives as they walked away from the festivities. "All jokes aside, it's good to see you," said Carl. "How is everything? Your little boy, how old is he?" "He's four." "How long have you been married, Chaz?" "We've been married five years and a few months." "No disrespect to your wife or family, but I thought you and Lenora would marry. I mean you and she were made for each other." Chaz sighed deeply, and said, "Everyone did, including us. Things happen and when things don't go as you planned, you make the best of it." "I heard your wife is pretty, though." "Yes, my wife is, and you know her." "I know her?" Carl asked. "Sure you do. She used to play with us when you came to visit." "Remember it used to be you, me, Lenora, Madeline, Ricky and." "Ricky, Ricky," Carl said interrupting Chaz. "What is he doing now?" "He joined the Navy, and is in the South Pacific," replied Chaz. "Remember how your Grandfather used to say to him, "Ricky Stone, stay solid as a rock.

Don't let nobody turn you to the right and don't let nobody turn you to the left.''' The two old friends laughed. "I do, and that little piece of advice that Granddaddy gave him must have stuck. Ricky plans to buy Uncle Isaac's store and marry one of the resident girls." "Those are big dreams for a little Hill boy." "Ricky was destined for bigger and better things," said Chaz. "Like you my friend," said Carl. "Like me Carl? I am struggling to make heads or tails over what to do with my life." "Your life, hey man you have a pretty woman, you have a fine son, you have your ministry and you've got your family." "Praise God, I know, but being married to a pretty woman is not enough when there is no love." Chaz could not believe the words flowing from his mouth. He kept his emotions controlled and hadn't shared his thoughts or feelings about his failed marriage with anyone. "I remember this place, Chaz. This is where we would come as kids and talk about what we wanted to do with our lives." "Yes, it is. Lenora and I continued coming here to share and talk about any and everything. It became a special place for us. It was our place to be alone. Unfortunately, this is also the place where my son was conceived. Excuse me, let me rephrase. This is the place where my son was conceived. He is not an unfortunate mistake he is my blessing, my shining star despite my relationship with his mother. No my son is not the unfortunate part, having sex with his mother was." Carl couldn't have imagined his friend's misery, given one thousand years. The woman he married must certainly be wretched, he thought. "Chaz, I am sorry to see you down on yourself this way. I know I haven't seen you for years and I don't mind you sharing these things with me, but I don't know what to say. I don't know what I can do to help you." "An ear, Carl is fine. I can't believe I've shared my deepest thoughts and feelings with anyone else except, God." "You have your father to share with. Haven't you shared these things with him?" "I can't bring myself to share with him because he is living in that particular hell with me." "What do you mean?" Chaz sat down on the rock under the dogwood tree next to where Carl was standing, where he and Lenora carved their names in the center of a heart. Slowly rubbing his hand over his head, he straightened himself, and said, "She hates us. She hates me, our son, my parents and this community. The only relief we have is when she is away. We have the knowledge that she is having an affair, and this is not the first one." "Wait a minute, man? You mean to tell me that the woman you are married too, the mother of your son, a preacher's wife is cheating on you. You've got to be joshing me, Chaz?" Carl shook his head in disbelief. "I don't think I've ever heard of that before. I'm not saying it doesn't go on, I am sure it does. I can't imagine anything like that happening to anyone we know, especially to the likes of you. I mean, I know you and you would give anyone the shirt off your back. You ain't no punk either. I remember you could hold your own in a scrape. When those other little boys tried to tease and pick on you, me and Ricky would stand back and watch you beat them down. We had your back but we never had to jump in to save you. What kind of woman did you get mixed up with? What did she do, force you to take her? No one imagined you with anyone else except Lenora, what happened?" "It's like I said, it happened right here on this spot. I was in deep, deep thought, about Lenora. Her father had sent her to live with her Grandmother in New York. I missed my friend, I missed the only girl I had ever loved and who loved me. I tried to love my wife. I did everything I could to make our home a happy one. I removed all of the pictures of Lenora in our house from view. All were removed too, except the one in Daddy's study he refused to put it away. My wife never went into his study anyway. She says it makes her feel like God is in there and that's one room she wants to stay out of." "Man-oh-man, what did you get yourself into? Chaz, it is one thing I don't understand. If you were in deep thought about Lenora, how did this other girl get to you? "I was up here, Carl, in our spot minding my own business, lying on my back thinking private and passionate thoughts about the girl I love." "Passionate thoughts, you mean you were thinking about her in a manly way?" "Yes, if you want to put it that way. My eyes were closed as I sunk deeper and deeper into thought. The next thing I knew she was standing over me with her skirt raised to her waist." "Standing over you, Lenora?" "No. Lenora would never do anything like that before we were married. It was my wife, and to make a long story short, I closed my eyes and she became Lenora. I don't think I feel there is a need to go any further, except to say my son was conceived that very same evening. She once laughed in my face, and said, "How pitiful she had been to have planned to have a child by someone like me." She planned it and gave me details, step-by-step. Then she threw her wedding band at me, spat in my face and swore she would never have relations with me again. That was three years ago when she told me those things." "Wait a minute. You mean you are married to a woman that you sleep in the same bed with and you don't get no nooky?" "Carl, get no nooky, I don't see no nooky. Do you still think I have everything, Carl?" "Yes, I still do, Chaz. Only you would stick it out for your son and your parents to hold your family together. Me, shoot, I wouldn't have hit her, but I would have kicked her butt out into the street a longtime ago. Come on man, I don't like to see you like this. I haven't seen you for years, and I have brought you down," said Carl. "Don't think of it that way, I am more than happy to have gotten that off my chest. Who else at this time but you could I have shared it with?" Chaz said feeling at ease. The two young men stood and gave each other another hug and patted the other on the back. "I am glad you still trust me enough to share something so close to you, Chaz. Let's get back so that I can get a good look at this woman you married, and eat some more of that good cooking." "Yea, let's get back. Momma is probably losing her mind because she has lost one of her hosts." Carl wanted to tell his friend about his precious find. Too bad, he thought, he'll never experience the love I know with that old wife of his. He was curios to get a look at that thing he's married too and wondered what she looked like. "Speaking of women Carl, not mine of course, there are a lot of single church girls at the picnic," said Chaz. "I've noticed, said Carl, "but none of them compare to the one I've got." "The one you've got? You let me go on and on about my troubles and not once did you tell me that you had someone." "Yea, I do, and I've got big plans for us too." "That's alright, man. What are you trying to tell me? The next time I see you will be at your wedding?" "Yep. That's my plan." "I know you, if that's your plan than that's what is going to happen. I am looking forward to meeting the one that got you. She must be someone special." "She is Chaz, she is."

"Here comes the second round," said one of the elderly gentlemen standing around the table speaking with Bully. The men patiently watched as the women appeared with trays full of food and disappeared with empty trays only to reappear with full trays to and from the back door. "I don't know which is more inviting," said one of the younger men, "the food on the trays or what's carrying the trays. I have never seen so many pretty women in my life." "Me either, young fellow," said one of the older men. To Carl's surprise someone very familiar bearing a tray filled with cakes and cookies was coming in his direction. His heart leaped, when he saw Patty in the sundress she bought last weekend and modeled for him. Just as he began to call out to her he heard and saw a peculiarity. Chaz's son Joey calling out to his mother and Carl's pretty Patty walked over to the child saying, "What is it this time, Joey?" Pointing, Joey answered, "Momma, Lester didn't believe you were my mother because you're so pretty. He thought my mother was an ugly old witch. And he said, whenever he heard someone talk about you, they called you a witch." "Well Lester," Patricia said, "I am not a witch. What do you say to that?" Lester staring down at his feet could only utter, "Nothing Mam," before running as fast as he could in the opposite direction. Joey followed as fast as his little feet could carry him, yelling, "Hey Lester, wait for me!" A witch, Patricia thought, I bet a lot of people want to replace that "w" with a "b". She chuckled, turning to make her way back into the house. Out of the corner of her eye she caught a glimpse of something familiar. It was shadowy, and she could just make out the outline of the physique. "No, it can't be!" Patricia said to herself stepping back, fully turning and looking to her left. It was, Carl!! What was he doing here? Patricia thought. Reluctant to move, she started toward him then stopped. Unable to move any closer to one another because of the multitude of guests massing about them they locked glances. His head reeling, Carl wanted to reach out for her, but couldn't. His hopes, his dreams, his desires were dissolving before his eyes. This is Chaz's wife, she is the mother of his son, she is the wretched woman, was his summarization. "Why is Carl staring at me like that, hasn't he come to take me away?" She asked herself. "What is he thinking about, what is he doing?" He stood staring at Patricia, paralyzed. Just then his father touched the small of his back, and said, "Have you met, Patricia Carter, Chaz's wife?" Carl looked back at his father, his eyes filling with tears, and said, "I am ready to go, Dad." "Sure son, if you say so," said Bully. Without saying their goodbyes, father and son rapidly darted between the hedges that separated the driveway from the expansive lawn. Buy the time they reached the car, Carl was sobbing. Bully handed his handkerchief to his son, stepped back and shoved his hand into his pants pockets. Patiently he waited for his son to compose himself. "Pop, you knew?" "Yes, I knew. I saw the two of you together about a month ago." "Dad, why did you let me go through this? Why didn't you say something to me?" "Carl, what could I have said to you? What was I to say? If you had been in my shoes, what would you have said?" "I don't know, something, anything. What should I do, Dad?" "What does your heart tell you to do?" "Well, Dad," Carl said as he blew then wiped his nose on the handkerchief. "My head say's to grab her by the throat and ring her neck. My heart feels sorry for her." "Although, I agree with the head, for right now, Carl, I'd go with the heart."

"He's leaving!" Patricia's mind screamed. She had to catch Carl before he reached the end of the driveway and turned onto the main road. Calculating her next moves, she put the empty tray on the table in the kitchen. Maneuvered her way, unnoticed, through the horde of chattering women in the kitchen, passed through the dining room to the foyer then out the front door. She could never reach him amongst the hundreds of people and parked cars in the back and side yards. She had to cross the front yard and make her way through the parked cars, then catch him before he drives away. He'll understand my side of the story…I know he will, she thought. Her heart and mind were racing when she reached her destination. Clutching her chest, she tried to catch her breath and find words to say. If Carl hadn't looked both ways before turning right onto the main road, he would have missed seeing her standing to his left at the edge of the driveway. Bully knew that this was a true test for his son. He lowered his head, held his breath and whispered, "Lord your will be done." Carl looked at Patricia and began to move his lips. No words came out. With that one glance, he recalled every pitiless and vile intention he had executed against a woman. There was more than one way to hurt a person, a woman, than by hitting them. Carl's heart was broken. He had received his reckoning. Clearing his throat, he said, "Goodbye, Patricia." Again, he looked both ways, stuck his left arm out of the open window, bent his arm upward and made a right turn onto the main road. His father silently thanked the Lord for a safe trip home, and new life with his son.

Patricia left standing at the edge of the driveway couldn't believe what had taken place. Was she truly awake, did Carl drive away? Is he coming back? What should I do? Where can I go? Doesn't he love me? What was he doing here? How, what, why? The questions kept flooding her mind, as she slowly wiggled her way back through the parked cars towards the house. She knew where she was but she was lost. She was lost in the front yard of her home, their home, the Carter's home.

Chapter Nineteen
HOME AT LAST

Ricky had traveled all over the world. Nowhere in his travels did he remember a sky as blue or the air as sweet as in his home, Kendal Grove. Overjoyed to say the least, he had finally met his mother, Eugina, and he wanted the whole wide world to know. Like a magnet to metal his heart drew him first to the home of the Carter's. He needed to have a talk with Reverend Joe before sharing the news of finding his mother with his love, Madeline. He needed to talk to him about more than filling in the blanks of his life. He also wanted advice on how to break the news of finding his mother to his father, Macabee. Ricky had toyed with the notion of not telling his father anything. Why, should I tell him that I found her, where she is or how she is doing? He thought. On the other hand there was another part of Ricky that wanted to bolt into his father's house to acclaim his newly found treasure. But at all costs he wanted to avoid confrontation with Macabee. In his heart he knew that not telling him about her was not the Christian thing to do. Besides Ricky didn't hate his father he just didn't understand him. He could only recall one conversation with his father. Other than that his father gave him short commands: "It's time to get up. Come eat your breakfast. Don't forget your lunch. Come eat your dinner. Do your chores. It's your bedtime. If Reverend Joe said, "do it," than do it." Ricky couldn't remember if his father had ever called him by name. Afraid to ask anyone about his mother's absence for fear of retribution from his father, the questions mounted over the years. It was obvious that Reverend Joe had a lot to do with his upbringing, and he was sure he had the answers to his questions. He was determined to get answers to his questions before he could continue with his life.

Using his secrete knock on the Carter's front door brought a scream of joy from Bertha. She hadn't seen her other boy since the day he left Kendal Grove for military service in the Navy. "Ricky Stone!" She screamed tearing open the front door. "Hug me boy!" Tears streamed down her cheeks, as she held him in her arms. "Looka who's here," said Joe. "Your other boy is home," said James shaking Ricky's shoulder. "Come on in here, boy," said Reverend Joe as he extended his hand. "Look at you, a grown man for sure. How long of a spell are you home for?" "This is it, I'm home for good," said Ricky. "I thought about it for a longtime and I have it all planned out." "Wedding plans I hope," said Bertha. "Why you rushing the boy?" said James. "Boy? This boy you say, is a twenty-three year old man, who has been all over the world," said Joe. Ricky smiled. "Like I said, I have made a lot of plans and a wedding is in there too." "Praise the Lord," said Bertha. "You see, I know I didn't help raise no heathen. My other boy is now a man," she said heading back into the kitchen, wiping her moist eyes with the bottom of her apron. "Where is Chaz?" Ricky asked. He's been over in Bricktown for a few days working on his ministry," said Joe, "and he's due back this way early this evening. Your best buddy has built up a strong ministry over there and its neighboring communities. Those people had no direction and needed help. I'm talking about worse than some folks upon the Hill and Picker's Woods combined. On top of that they couldn't read nor write. Praise God, Chaz has done wonders for those folk. He got people from the Hill and the Woods to go over to Bricktown and help. They've even built a church. Your father has been most influential with his carpentry skills." "Excuse me sir," said Ricky. "Did you say my father?" "Yes, I did." "Macabee has been a wizard when it comes to contributing his expertise. Can't nobody beat your daddy when it comes to a hammer and nail." "Ricky, are you staying for dinner?" Bertha asked leaning through the kitchen door? "Yes, if I can?" Ricky replied. "If you can, boy, if you weren't a grown man, I would pop those lips for you saying that. I can't believe you said anything like that Ricky Stone?" After dinner James excused himself saying, "Ricky my boy, it is the second Saturday of the month and I have to meet with the Men's Choir. I hate to run out on you like this, but you understand." That's o.k. Reverend James, because I wanted to spend some time talking with Reverend Joe anyhow." "That worked out fine," said James leaving to attend the Men's choir rehearsal. "So you needed some time with me, Ricky? Let's go into the living room and have a seat, so you can tell me what's on your mind." "I want to thank you, Reverend Joe." "Why are you thanking me, Ricky?" "I am thanking you for several things: sending me the letter for one, and for helping me to grow as a man. You can stop me at anytime, Reverend Joe." "For what, Ricky, I am basking in the compliments." They burst into laughter. "Don't stop now. Isn't there anything else you can think of to thank me for?" "Isn't that enough?" "O.k.," said Reverend Joe adjusting himself in his easy chair. "How is my Goddaughter?" "She is your Goddaughter?" Ricky asked surprised. Reverend Joe moved to the edge of his easy chair. "Yes, your mother is my Goddaughter?" "Why is it that you never told me before?" "You act like I never planned to tell you." "Answer my question, how is my Goddaughter? I haven't seen her in four years." "Reverend Joe, you knew where my mother was all the time?" "Of course I did. How do you think she got there?" Ricky looked puzzled as he eagerly awaited each word to proceed from the old minister's mouth. "You see, Ricky, your father was nothing short of a hellion. The best things in his life were you, your mother and his parents. I can't say he never loved his parents, but I can say that he didn't respect them or himself. I remember when your mother and father were married. Your father's mother said to your mother's parents, "Ya'll know we love Eugina as our own, but God himself only knows what she sees in Macabee. She's sweet and such a lady. I was happy the day he told me he wanted to marry her, but the boy was so used to hanging around those wild Wynn boys and their rough women. The kind of people we would never let set foot in our house. He saw goodness in Eugina and we loved her at first site. Marrying her was the best decision he ever made in this life thus far. I love that girl as my own, but I can't make any promises for my son." That's quite a load to hear from your in-laws on the day of your daughter's wedding. But your father's mother was one who spoke from the heart. Macabee was bad enough before his parents died in the bus accident. Afterwards, Joe shook his head from side-to-side, he became out of control. He began beating your mother at whim. It seemed he was taking his anger, despair, and all of I don't know what else out on Eugina. All of whatever was in his stinking soul was being directed at your mother. It was though he was trying to punish her for loving him." "My grandparents died in the bus accident?" "Yes, my wife and one of Lenora's grandmothers, and one of her grandfathers who came from New York to go on the bus trip with us. Ricky, I didn't know you weren't told these things." "No, I really didn't know." "I guess people assumed I knew, so no one ever spoke about it to me." "What did Macabee say about your mother?" "Nothing, he never mentions her name. It was if she never existed after she left. Why did she leave, Reverend Joe?" "She didn't want to leave without you. She had no choice but to leave, or she probably wouldn't be alive today. Your father beat her bad that last time. He broke her nose, two ribs and her arm. That beating was because he went to strike you, and she shielded you. When she went to the hospital you came to live with us. You were about four years old, you don't remember that?" "I remember a little about her but not that." "I am glad you don't because you were such a little boy and what a terrible thing for a little child to remember. You were a good boy, a real nice child. Your father made no attempt to visit your mother while she was in the hospital. So after a few days I made up my mind what to do. When she was released from the hospital I took her to where you found her in Pennsylvania. The Goodwin's are good people and sincerely cared for your mother, the lovely creature that she is, from the start. After her divorce was final, the eldest son of the Goodwin's married her, and his people became her people. Did she share with you her photograph album?" "No, she didn't." "She should have. Do you recall whenever we took pictures of you we would say, hold it for another one?" "Yes sir, I do." "The first snapshot was for her. I've kept her abreast of you since the day she left. When I got your mother settled in Pennsylvania and returned home, I took my gun." "You have a gun, Reverend Joe?!" "Close your mouth, Ricky, and let me finish. Like I said, I took my gun with me to your house. I knew he was in there because I could hear the radio playing. I kicked the door open, and there he was standing in the middle of that filthy living room looking at me wide-eyed, with some crazy looking woman with her hair sitting all over her head. He came at me like he wanted to fight. I grabbed him around the neck, and his mouth sprang open. So I placed the mussel of the gun in his mouth. Then I told that thing of a woman to get out. She grabbed up her little things, and ran past me so fast I felt a breeze. She didn't care about your father, because she didn't scream, look back, or nothing. I then said, "You almost killed your wife because she was like your mother, a real mother to her son. Mavis won't be coming back. Your son who is the seed of my best friend is safe in my home for now, but he will be coming back to live with his father in this house. This house will be kept spotless like the kind of home you were raised in. He will eat three meals a day and he will be kept clean. If you attempt to find your wife or consider placing a hand on Ricky, I will kill you…slowly." I then removed the gun from his mouth turned around and walked home praying every step of the way and asking God's forgiveness for what I'd done." "I don't understand, Reverend Joe My father never backed down from anyone else, why did he back down from you?" Joe slid back into his easy chair and sighed, then hesitated before he spoke. "Many years ago when I was a young man, and my son and your daddy were little, tiny boys, as a matter of fact both of them were beginning to walk. There was this man, a white man, who used to do horrible things to little Negro girls. What he would do is grab them when they were alone playing. Doing little girl things, picking flowers, skipping, singing or playing with their dolls, tending to their own business. Well, he hurt two little girls." "Why, didn't someone stop him?" "Now Ricky, you know how it goes. Some of us got together and took the matter to the Sheriff because everyone knew who was hurting those little girls.

The Sheriff knew who was doing it too, so we were ignored and told to go home. Because they were little Negro girls the white folk didn't care, and white law didn't apply. If anything bad happens to a Negro for some reason or another white folk think they deserve it. After the second time, I couldn't stand by and keep hoping for change, so I started watching for him. Low and behold, there he was one afternoon creeping across Willow's field like a wild animal seeking its prey. Willow's field has that high grass where those wildflowers grow. Remember that field also separates Kendal Grove from Franklin. Anyway, I got down and waited in the tall grass until he got real close to me, then I slowly stood up, because he carried a gun and I didn't want to startle him. Then I casually asked, "Can I help you?" He looked me straight in the eye and said, "Get away from me you dirty black nigger," and began to walk passed me. I then said, "Ain't no little girls around here this afternoon." He turned around to me and said, "What did you say to me you smart ass, black nigger? I will kill you where you stand, and then kill your fat, ugly, black mammy." I looked straight into his eyes and said, "I ain't got no mammy, but I do have a mother. Maybe you wanted a mammy and that's why you mess around with little Negro girls." Just then he reached for his gun he kept tucked in the front of his belt. He pointed the gun in the middle of my face and pulled the trigger. The gun jammed, I walked over to him, snatched it out of his hands, and hit him with it, square in the middle of his face." Ricky sat paralyzed, as he watched Joe and took in every. "There he was lying on the ground looking up at me pleading, "don't shoot me, please, don't shoot me." Look at this pitiful piece of cracker trash, I thought to myself. I dropped the gun and began walking away from him. The next thing I knew he was up on his feet calling me everything except a child of God. I turned to face him and he pointed the gun in my face again. I knew for sure I was gone. All I could see was the gun pointing in my face and his lips moving. I don't remember hearing anything except a little voice inside me saying, "Help me Lord." He pulled the trigger and again the gun jammed. I snatched it away from him, pointed it in his face and still didn't pull the trigger. I watched again as he begged me not to kill him. This time he was on his knees saying, "Please don't hurt me." "What happened?" Ricky asked. "I unloaded the gun and threw it a few feet past his head, turned around and walked away. A few days later he was found dead over in Parsons County. I won't say I was sorry he was dead. But I did thank and praise God that I wasn't the one to take his life. You see, Ricky, I found out later that some of the fellows had witnessed what took place between me and that white man. So when he was found dead some folk took it upon themselves to believe that I killed him. No matter how I tried to deny it people still believed that I had killed him. Your Grandfather, my best friend, believed that I did it. We never discussed it but when someone would bring it up he would sit back and give me that look of his. That Grandfather of yours was really something. You would have liked him. Not just because he was your Grandfather, but he was a good man. The point that I am making is that your father grew up believing I had killed a white man." "I understand," said Ricky. "My father felt that if you were the type of man that would kill a white man, you wouldn't hesitate to kill him." "You've got it," said Joe.

Ricky changing the subject asked, "Sir, you'll never guess who I saw on the way back to the ship in Harlem, Bailey Watts." "Old Bailey, so that's where he wound up? What's he doing there?" "From what he told me, he's working as a director at Hollis Funeral Home." "Is he ever planning to come back this way?" "I can't say for sure. Let me put it the exact way he told me. "I miss Kendal Grove and sometime I miss my wife and son, but I don't miss her ways or her sister. I still love my wife, but at the same time I can't stand her."" "Did you tell him he was a grandfather?" "No, I didn't know. Madeline didn't write to me about that." "He has two grandsons. Victoria didn't acknowledge them, because her boy had them by Pickle Johnson, Lippy's sister. The other day she came over insisting that one of us, James or me, marry Hector and Pickle, because she no longer wanted to be a Grandmother to bastard children. That woman never ceases to amaze me. James is going to marry them next Saturday morning in a private ceremony."

Reverend Joe had more to share with Ricky before he set off to Macabee's. "There is one more thing before you go see your father," he said. "Madeline wrote you about the new fellow that came to town from New York, who is courting Juniper, right? The reason he came to town was to take a look around to find a site for a new bank." "We'll have a bank in Kendal Grove?" Ricky asked. "That's right Kendal Grove will have its own bank right next to Howard's Apparel. That fellow that's courting Juniper is the Manager of the Savings and Loan Bank. Now, the Owner of the Lumber Yard, Jacob Aldor, is also the owner and President of the bank. Jacob has selected the Board of Directors for the bank and there is one seat still vacant. Let's see there is James, Isaac, Chaz, Winton and you're not going to believe this one, Lippy Johnson, excuse me Lawrence Johnson." "What?" "Oh yeaaaa. Lippy, has done quite well for himself. After his daddy died he took that old horse and wagon and began transporting people from the Hill to work in Franklin and to the railroad station. He also worked part-time at the general store with Isaac." "Yes sir. I knew that because Madeline wrote me about it." "From there he got a truck, the kind you load hey on. He fixed it up so he could tote more people back and forth. At present he has four cabs and a passenger bus for excursions. I tell you, it's not what it used to be like around here. The people on the Hill don't live like heathens in little shanties anymore. You wouldn't recognize Pickers Woods partly due to jobs at the Lumber Yard and the President's better road projects. Ethel and her husband built a real nice home up in those Woods. That Ethel did real well for herself in Parsons. She worked at Mrs. Bee Jansen's House of Beauty, got her Cosmetology License and opened her own shop next to the bank. Brother Dan was ordained, has his own church in the Woods and married a gal who lived down the road from him. She's ugly and is a little rough around the edges, but everyone can't be like our Annie and Ethel. Dan built a nice house too, similar to ours. They say, "The best form of flattery is imitation." Now we've got way off the subject. Ricky, what I really wanted to talk to you about was me asking James to recommend you for the last seat on the Bank's Board." "Me? Why don't you take the seat, Reverend Joe?" "No." It's time for the young men to take over. What am I asking you for? The seat is yours. Go on about your business boy, I'll talk to you later. And welcome home."

Ricky was more than surprised to see his portrait, in full dressed uniform, on the mantle over the fireplace. It took him forever to make the decision to send the portrait to his father. For weeks after he sent it he half-heartedly awaited the daily mail for the envelope to be returned unopened. After it had not been returned he suspected that it had gotten lost in the mail or Macabee had received it and tore it into little pieces and burned the little pieces in the fireplace. "What you doing home?" Macabee asked. "I am home for good, Pop," said Ricky. "Where are you going to stay?" "Pop, I'd figured to stay with you until I get all my stuff in order." "What stuff?" Macabee asked as he sat down in his arm chair. "I've got plans, Pop. Some plans I have been thinking on for a few years." "Like what?" "You know the regular stuff...get into business for myself, buy a home and get married." "Business, home, marriage, and who's going to marry a big-eyed boy like you?" He said laughingly to his son. "You got big eyes, and someone married you." "Yea, someone did, but that was a long while ago." "I saw her, Pop." "Saw who?" Macabee asked lifting himself from his chair. He knew exactly who his son had seen, and dreaded this day since Eugina left Kendal Grove. Deep in his heart he hoped that he could be wrong and it wasn't Eugina he had seen. Macabee was a changed man who had left the obnoxious, narcissistic and ignorant acting jackass behind. His longstanding strategy not to hold conversations with his boy to avoid questions regarding his mother or her whereabouts had come to an abrupt end with no warning. Ricky was no longer a boy. He was an intelligent and articulate, well traveled man. Macabee tried to leave the room but before he could, Ricky said, "My Mother." Macabee stopped in his tracks. "Pop she is beautiful, she is wonderful and such a lady." Ricky censing his father's uneasiness smiled and asked, "How in the world did you with your big old eyes get someone like mother?" Macabee looked at his son, relieved that Ricky did not place blame. "What you talking about, how did I get?" He said jokingly. "Shoot boy, I am still getting. I got woman falling at my feet." "Yea pop, but how did they get there?" Ricky asked. "What did you have to do to get them to fall? Push or trip them?" They broke into laughter. The way only a father and son can laugh together. Ricky could not recall a time in his life when he experienced his father's folly. This was truly an amazing time for him.

It was a great homecoming and a time of firsts. He had completed his tour of duty, found his mother after years apart from her, and was engaged to be married to a wonderful woman. He felt welcome in his home for the first time in his life and his father was laughing and joking with him. Ricky was certain that on this day there was nothing he could not accomplish. His whole world had come together for him and from this day on he could fail at nothing.

Chapter Twenty
IT'S OVER

"He has left me," Patricia mumbled. He's gone, and that no good Ricky Stone, thinking he's so cute in his little Navy uniform, had a nerve to say that he would never want me now. After the way he used to look at me and run after me when we were kids. I know and everybody knows that he wants me. He said, "I had become nothing but a piece of drunken trash"...he said that to me? He said that the trash I tried to run from, on the Hill, was what I had become. Time and again she repeated the same thing, trying to sedate her pain of abandonment and loneliness with alcohol. She couldn't decide what hurt the most, her head, her heart or her entire body. There was no one left who would dare try to love her. Even her father's brother the last of her close blood relatives, Uncle Paul was dead and he would have been a good drinking buddy. "Doctor, what can you do for this pain?" Patricia asked Doctor Mitchell. "Not a thing Patricia, nothing," Dr. Mitchell said. "What do you mean nothing?" "There is nothing I can give you for a hangover except the advice to stop drinking." As the doctor was putting his instruments back into his bag, Patricia called him a "quack," then slid off the bed onto the floor. He helped her from the floor, and gave her a good shaking to get her full attention. "Patricia, look at me," he said. "Why, don't you go away for a while? I remember your Grandmother had some people in Virginia. Let me get in touch with them so you can go for a visit." Patricia wiggled out of his grip, plopped back onto the bed and said, "No! I don't want to waste my time visiting those no teeth, ugly hillbillies." "Teeth or no teeth, I remember them being very fine folk." "I don't care, I can't stand them! They probably still don't have indoor plumbing." "If they don't, get out there and get back into the old time country feeling. I recollect, your Grandmother was quite fond of them." "No she wasn't, she only tolerated them." "I know that not to be true of Minnie Haynes. If she invited them to her home it was because she wanted them there. You really need to consider going to visit them. I think the time away would be good for you." Patricia lied back down, and turned away from the doctor. She then decided to test the doctor by turning over and pretending to stretch her shapely legs. Pulling back the covers she shoved her vulva up, inches from his face. Appalled by her indecent behavior, in a gruff tone he said, "Patricia that is uncalled for! I have seen plenty raw butts long before I saw yours. Don't forget I delivered your son!" She closed her legs, rolled her eyes at him, and turned over leaving her backside in full view as he left the room. Exiting her bedroom in a huff, he slammed the bedroom door behind him. "What is it Frank?" asked Bertha. "Bertha, it's the same as always, she has to stop drinking?" The Doctor shook his head, while cleaning his spectacles and trying to contain his anger. "But Frank, she was moaning as if she were in great pain." "Excuse me, my dear Bertha that is how most drunkards sound after bingeing for days on end." "If alcohol makes you feel that way than why continue to drink it?" "I don't have an answer for you Bertha, not this time. I have other calls to make I'll be leaving you now." "Thank you, for coming by this morning Frank. How much is that…$2.50, I owe you?" She said, reaching into her change purse. "Here you are, and have a wonderful day." "Thank you, Bertha, and the same to you."

When Bertha entered the bedroom she could not believe that Patricia would bare herself like that for anyone to see, if they walked into the bedroom. The woman had no shame, she thought. "Patricia, Patricia." she called at her bedside. Patricia, asleep, didn't answer her call. Infuriated by her drunkenness, and lack of common decency, Bertha with her open hand, hit Patricia on her bare bottom, making a loud popping sound. Awakened by the sound and the stinging sensation of the blow, she instantly sat up and turned in the direction of Bertha. "Pull your covers over you," said Bertha. "Do you want your son to walk in and see you this way?" "They ain't here," Patricia replied.

"Just the same, your nakedness is precious, only for God and your husband to see. Get up, Young Lady!" Bertha snapped. "Don't you know that sin will bring you nothing but death?" Patricia unflinching, Bertha tossed the covers over her and left the room before she said anything else to her daughter-in-law. It was difficult to maintain a civil attitude and tongue to Patricia. Walking down stairs and a few feet down the hall she entered the study to take away James' lunch tray. "How is she?" he asked. "The same as before the doctor said. She's hung over. What happened to her girlfriend, Carla? Those were such nice quite days when she visited her. I was thinking about getting some of that poison we discussed the other day." James looking at his wife over the rim of his glasses asked, "You mean for Mrs. Lawson's rat problem?" "Mrs. Lawson's rat, what about our rat?" "Mrs. Carter, I think you have been reading too many mystery novels." "Oh Lord, please forgive me," said Bertha. She than sat down on the lap of her husband, placing her hand in his. "He does, he does darling," he said, softly kissing her neck. "I have asked the Lord for so much tolerance," she said sighing. "James, I sometime wonder if He will ever run out? For several years, we looked at our situation and refused to believe it was a problem, and that one day everything would come together for her and our son. But now honey, I have to see it for what it is, it's a problem. Yet, through it all, I continue to give our God the praise. I've never taken what you and I have together for granted, nowadays it means much more to me. I love you James and I know you love me. I have always known that you've loved me. Well, let me refrain, not always." "What are you talking about Bertha, when did I not love you?" "When we were children, you used to do the meanest things to me. Throw stones at me and put bugs down the back of my dress. Remember the time you put a dead tadpole in my lunch pail?" "I did all that because I liked you. Some boys are that way. And I would have kept doing it, if your mother had not told your mother that I was being mean to you." "I never knew your mother had a talk with my mother." "She sure did." "What did your mother say?" "It wasn't so much of what mother had to say, it was what my father said." "What did he say?" "When my mother was scolding me about picking on you Poppa spoke up and said, "He is doing that because he likes her." I remember smiling because he understood what I had told no one, and it made be blush. Then he said, "Some boys are simple like that. You knuckle head, do you see me running around throwing stones at your mother, pushing on her, or any mess like that? And I really love her. If you want to put something in her lunch pail, put a flower in it, or a slice of your mother's chocolate cake or some candy. You are my son and you are to be a gentleman, like me." Then he rubbed the back of my head and said, "We will never have to have this talk again, right?" Of course I agreed, and stuck to it. I can still remember the first time I saw you." "Oh James, honestly, you are making this up." "No, really, I am not making this up. We were little things we couldn't have been much older than six or seven years old." "You can remember way back then?" "Yes, a few things. You and some other little girls were in the Willow's field picking wild flowers. I remember seeing you and wanting to pick every flower in that field and give them to you." "Than what did you do?" "I started running as fast as I could toward you, I pushed you down, and kept running." They burst into laughter. "See James, you were so mean to me." "I didn't mean it. I didn't know what I was doing at the time. I can't believe you don't remember that," he said. "You sat there and cried." "I was only a baby, James." "Joe in a teasing mood, opened the door to the study, and asked, "What are you two doing all lovey-dovey in the middle of the day? Can't you all find something else to do?" "Aw Poppa, I can remember you and mother being all lovey-dovey when I was a boy." "Yea, but we didn't have radio and Fishing Magazines. All we had was each other." They all laughed. "Let me get on my way and leave ya'll alone." When Joe closed the door, Bertha turned to James, and said, "Honey, I want to pray for forgiveness." James led them in prayer, "Father we come to you with open hearts this afternoon, with prayers of thanksgiving. We asked your forgiveness for our short comings. We thank you Father for the life of bounty you have bestowed upon us. We thank you for your grace and your mercy.

We thank you for the health, happiness and peace of this household no matter what the circumstances. You are still God and Lord of our lives. We humbly ask forgiveness for our unbridled tongues, and wicked thoughts toward another. We asked this blessing in the name of your precious son, Jesus the Christ our Lord and Savior and we both say, Amen." "Thank you honey, I'll clear away these dishes and let you get back to your sermon." "Oh yea, and baby," James said to Bertha, "I think you should cut back on those mystery novels." "Me too honey, me too," she replied leaving the study.

Chapter Twenty-One
A BRAND NEW LIFE

Sonny went to Parsons using the back roads. The old farm road was a bit out of his way but he could move faster because the road was less traveled. The houses on this road were five to six miles apart and with all the open country the view was also better. The drive gave him ample time to waiver in his conversation with himself and the Lord. "I sure would like to buy us a place like one of these some day," he said to himself. "I could teach my boys how to till the land and raise crops. We would have chickens, hogs and a few cows. Our land would feed us. I could also teach them how to drive and service our equipment, trucks and tractors. We could harvest and haul our own produce. We wouldn't have to pay anyone to do that for us which would put more money in our pockets. Annie could have her own garden like she does now but a much bigger one. I know not one thing would ripen before its time in that garden. Come to think of it, I don't know if a bigger garden would be a good idea or not? Annie might can herself to death, because that is one canning woman. It's a miracle she hasn't found a way to can weeds or dirt, but that's my Annie. Maybe, I could find some land for sale with apple and other fruit trees? Nobody makes an apple pie like my Annie. Naw, buying Reverend Joe's old house, directly across the street from Momma Bertha, will suit us fine. That was a good idea of Reverend Joe to sale me his house after his tenants moved on. Lord, thank you, for not giving up on me. I could have missed realizing, and enjoying what I had at home. I didn't have to go anywhere else to look for an exciting life because it was already there and I couldn't see it. It would have never crossed my mind old Earl Case would have a part in waking me up out of state of confusion. I truly thought I was happy before running with that woman but the last six months with Annie and my boys have proven to be the best time I've ever had in my life. Thank you Lord, thank you," he said. Sonny was so grateful and overjoyed that he pressed harder on the accelerator and shifted the gear into fourth. He wanted to get to Parsons faster to complete his mission, and return to Kendal Grove to his wife and children as soon as possible.

On his return home he began singing the blues: "I'm a grown man and ain't got time for no more fights. Baby, let me cook for you. Let me rub you down with my special seasoning like I do my meat going on the spit fire. I can spit and I've got fire – let me play with your love. Then I'll lick my fingers like I do the sauce of my hot bar-b-que. Yea, come here baby let me play with your love." Sweet, sweet Annie I know you don't like that nasty song but I'm singing it and thinking of you baby. Engulfed in his thoughts about teaching Annie to dance, he ran over the twisted piece of metal in the middle of the road. BANG sounded the right rear tire bursting. The truck abruptly jerked veering to the right of the road then to the left and than again to the right before coming to rest on the side of the road. After Sonny got out of the truck to examine the extent of the damage to his precious cargo, he noticed there was no spare tire. He surveyed the rows and rows of cornfields on both sides of the road and realized there had not been a person or a house in site for several miles. Sonny back tracked to where he heard the blast and there he found a large piece of sharp metal that looked as if it had once been apart of a plow. What fool would have left this right in the middle of the road? Should he walk back three miles to get to the last farm house he passed, only to find they don't have a telephone? Or won't let a Negro use the one they've got or should I walk the ten miles back to Parsons County? Sonny opted to walk straight past the farm house and go back ten miles to the Parsons County line. There he hoped to find Pettie at his garage to buy a new tire and use his telephone. When he reached the garage, Pettie was nowhere to be found. Desperate to contact someone in Kendal Grove he thought about using the telephone in the drug store but the telephone booth was for white's only. He'd have to walk another fifteen miles to reach the Negro drug store in the city of Parsons. From a distance he saw Pettie returning to his garage. Pettie was white but the color of ones skin did not bother him. He didn't care what color a man's skin was as long as his money was green. So White's and Negro's alike catered to his filling station's automobile repair shop. People catered to the station not only because of his lack of bias or off kilter sense of humor but because the next filling and service station was located miles away. Explaining the situation, Pettie gave Sonny and his new tire, and a ride back to the truck. Sonny was more than appreciative because he dreaded the ten mile walk back rolling the new tire all the way. Off they went in Pettie's raggedy pick-up truck to change the flat. The transaction moved so swiftly that Sonny forgot to place a call to Kendal Grove to make known his delay.

"Thanks for your help, Pettie," said Sonny. "You're welcome, Sonny," Pettie said. "Hey, we go way back," Pettie said attempting to wipe the dirt from his hands with the filthy oil stained pocket rag. With the looks of the rag and Pettie's hands, Sonny couldn't tell if he was wiping the dirt off or on his hands. "If it wasn't for you, I would have drowned in that gully when we were little things. None of the other white boys I was playing with jumped in to save me, when my leg cramped. And there you were, the little nigger boy, we used to pick on. I never forgot that, and you're the reason I do business with everybody." Sonny had forgotten about saving Pettie from drowning when they were children. "Thanks, again," said Sonny. The two men shook hands, got into their trucks and drove off in opposite directions.

Chapter Twenty-Two
SONNY AIN'T HERE

"Hell no, Sonny ain't here!" Patricia screamed. "Now, let me ask you Annie, why do you look like a plucked-headed chicken? You are a bald head, little, pale, skinny looking thing. You're nothing but a whole lot of yellow gone to waste. That's what you are, Annie Potts. You ain't no kind of woman that's why your husband is off somewhere else with another woman. And she looks like a real woman, because I know her, and she's pretty like me. She has got a face, she has a good body, and she has hair and skin smoother than anything you have ever seen before. If I was a man, I would never come home to your little, skinny, ass either. Look at you, in that old, ugly, hand-me-down dress. You really think you all dressed up, and looking good, with your raggedy brats? Bitch, please! Your husband ain't here. I heard him tell Chaz this morning that he was going over to Parsons, and he ain't coming back. Get your little, ugly, yellow ass off my porch and stay the hell out of this house. Go head home you little, plucked-headed chicken."

Abashed and engrossed in self pity, Annie backed down the front steps of the Carter's home away from Patricia's verbal onslaught. Suddenly she turned lost her balance falling face first onto the walkway. Patricia hysterically roared with laughter at her fall. Pulling herself up from the walkway, she wiped away her tears mixed with blood from the large gash under her right eye. Totally crushed, she walked toward the front gate. In horror of Patricia's maligning and the thought of Sonny slipping back into his old life style, after all of her prayers, she bolted from the pastor's yard feeling she had nothing else to live for. All of the joy she experienced in the last six months crashed with the words from Patricia's drunken mouth. She surmised that even though Patricia treated her with disdain and malice, she must know the truth about Sonny's whereabouts because she overheard their conversation. Sonny was more than two hours late, he was gone forever, she thought. Not knowing what to do, Annie ran, she ran as fast as she could to get away from Patricia's laughter. Absorbed in her self-hatred for being so stupid as to believe her husband could actually love her, and mad at God for giving her false hope, she didn't notice from a distance her children and Bertha walking towards her. "Momma, Momma!" the boys cried out to Annie. Their cries were drowned out by the thundering sorrows reechoing in her mind, she kept running. Bertha sensing dread gathered the boys together and sped toward her house only to find Patricia drunk, laughing and murmuring to herself on the front porch. As they got closer to Patricia, Bertha's stomach churned when she smelled the foul stench of alcohol and body odor. She could only make out a few words Patricia was saying, "Little plucked-headed chicken, your man ain't never coming back to you." Thank God, she thought. Little Joey was in Bricktown with his father. Bertha, hurried the boys into the house and clamed herself, before posing questions to her daughter-in-law. "Is that what you told, Annie?" she asked. Patricia standing from her chair, placed her face in front of Bertha's face and said, "Yea that's exactly what I told her, the truth! I am sick of all of you buzzing around that no good trash and her little piss-ass brats. Acting like she is honey." Patricia pointed to herself with a grand gesture, as if she were a politician running for office, and said, "All of that attention belongs to me. I'm the wife of your son, your daughter-in-law?" Bertha recalled the pain and grief the awful woman had caused so many people, good and decent people. The list was endless, she thought. There was no conscionable explanation why Patricia was so heartless. How could she be cruel to Annie, one who only expressed love and kindness to everyone? The juiced-up rabble offered nothing but pain, grief and embarrassment to me, my son, grandson, husband and father-in-law. Bertha was fed up with her cruelty and inconsideration, and with all of the strength she could muster, she slapped Patricia's face. Patricia, immediately fell to the porch floor. Not knowing exactly how she got there, but conscious of the increasing pain on the left side of her face, she began to wail loudly and uncontrollably. Looking down at her in complete disgust, Bertha walked over her to the screen door and told the boys to close and lock the doors. "Stay in the house until I get back, and don't let anyone in, not even Patricia. I am going to see about your mother," she said taking to the Hill on foot to Annie's house.

Good, thought Sonny, as he drove past the Pastor's house. The front door was closed and there were no cars in the driveway. To his knowledge everyone else was behind schedule too. He was sure within any minute Chaz would be returning from his ministry in Bricktown and the Reverends Joe and James would be returning from Parsons. He couldn't see Patricia passed out on the front porch, wedged between the wicker sofa and wall, hidden from passersby. Sonny was a new man with a new life, a new home and brand new furniture in the back of his truck. He anticipated the look on Annie's face when he proclaimed his love to her and all the people she cared about most in the world. It was going to be the way it should have been, he, Annie and their boys, a family.

Rounding the corner to the house on the Hill he heard a woman scream. Through the rickety screen door he could see Bertha standing inside, clutching her chest. Sonny parked the truck, skipped the porch steps and opened the screen door? Looking in the same direction as Bertha, he saw it too. His Annie was hanging by a sheet from the ceiling light fixture. "Annie, Annie!" He yelled, as he ran to her and tried to lift her body free from the makeshift noose. Trying over and over again to lift her body by the legs as if to unhook her from her bind was to no avail. "I have to cut her down! I have to cut her down!" He repeated, running to the kitchen to get Annie's favorite carving knife, a wedding gift from the Carter's. Bertha unable to speak or move was no help at all. Sonny grabbed the toppled table and placed it next to Annie's dangling feet. He stood on the table and wrapped one arm around Annie and used his free hand to cut the sheet. Before he could finish cutting the sheet the plastered ceiling gave way. Dropping the knife and falling backwards onto the floor, Annie fell into his arms. "Oh Annie," he cried, "I am here, I am here." Sonny gently kissed his wife's forehead and caressed her warm hand, as she lay in his arms for the last time. Bertha as if awakened from her worst nightmare, unaware that she was crying, took the noose from Annie's neck, wiped the plaster from her face, hugged and kissed them both and left Sonny alone to be with his wife.

"She fell into my arms, she fell into my arms," Sonny repeated sobbing. Annie's tearful boys, waiting to be reunited with their father, were outside of the Carter's house listening through an open window. From what Miles' young mind, the eldest of Annie's sons, could gather was that his father had found his mother dead, and somehow she fell into his father's arms. When the boys were allowed to enter the living room, Sonny, deeply sobbing, fell before them on his knees took them into his arms and said, "Your Momma is gone boys. Your Momma is gone." Before the boys could respond Bertha took them into the kitchen as Reverend Joe and his son James lifted Sonny onto his feet and sat him back in the chair.

As it was the custom in the small community of Kendal Grove, when a tragedy arose the residents congregated around the house of the preacher for the impeding news. Reverend James stepped out onto the front porch and spoke to the crowd. "For those of you who don't know, Annie Potts Jordon has passed away," he said. "My wife Bertha and Annie's husband Sonny found her. Sonny and the boys will be staying with us for a while. Everyone go home there is nothing else to tell you, except to pray that the Lord keep and protect Sonny and his boys and me and mine. Annie was like a daughter to my Bertha and me." As the crowd dispersed several shook their heads in disbelief. "That boy, ain't no more good," said one of the bystanders. "Who would have thought he would have acted this way when Annie passed on," said another bystander. "See I told you, only God knows what's in a man's heart," said another. "You sure did, you sure did, who would have ever thought it?" "What happened to her?" "All I know is what I heard Sonny say through the window.

Somehow wherever they found her, after she was dead, she fell into his arms. I don't know. She must have rolled into his arms." "I guess so." "It's sad though, too bad he didn't realize what a good woman he had early on. Ain't it?" "It sure is." "She was a real sweet girl and a good mother too." "You got that right, and everybody liked her." "Poor Bertha, Annie was like gold to her," another one said. Not fully understanding the cause or the circumstances of Annie's death, there was one thing certain, Bertha nor Sonny was at fault in her death. The other certainty, Annie never knew her worth.

"Chaz, what do you mean, what did I say to her?" Patricia said. "It's none of your damn business! It ain't my fault she ran away from here, half crazy. Get away from me and leave me the hell alone! I'm glad she is dead. Now you all can really make over your little precious, Annie. She can have the best funeral anyone has ever had in Kendal Grove."

Chapter Twenty-Three
SASSY'S IDENTITY

"You're my Aunt?" Sonny said, questioning what he heard from Sassy. "Yes, Sonny, I am your real mother's sister, Savanna," said Sassy. "Why, didn't you tell me?" "I didn't feel the need, until now. My past was something I wanted to forget." "Why tell me now?" "You and the boys need me, and I need you. I'm selling my place and moving into your new house with you and the boys. I've already discussed it with Joe, Earl and Estelle. So count it done."

As a young girl, Savanna Amsly was lovely, kind and considerate. She and her two sisters were much like their mother each with varying degrees of her traits. On the other hand her father, Ben, was an overbearing and bitter tyrant. Their home was happiest when he was at work, or on one of his two week long hunting or fishing trips. After school, her mother and sisters would spend what was left of the afternoon and early evening in gay conversations and cooking. The house was full of laughter each day until 6:30PM, on the dot, when all conversation would stop, because her father would soon enter the house. The table was set and dinner promptly began at 7:00PM. There was never any dinner conversation, nor did her father look at them while he ate. She wasn't exactly sure that her father knew what she or her sisters looked like. If he asked them a question, it was answered with a succinct "yes sir" or "no sir." There were no endearing words exchanged with him neither was he ever referred to as father, daddy or poppa, just sir. Unfortunately, her mother met an untimely death succumbing to cancer a week before Savanna's sixteenth birthday. With the death of their mother their father became bitterer. The girls were miserable not only because they were grieving the loss of their dear mother, but they were also grieving the loss of gladness in their home. Lucille, Savanna's eldest sister, although sickly, married a nice and handsome young man. Shortly, after their marriage he landed a job with the railroad. Unable to take his pregnant wife with him, he attempted to move her back home to her father. Ben flatly refused to be responsible for another man's child, even if it was his grandchild. Her mother's best friend, Estelle, stepped-in and insisted Lucille move with her in Parsons. Three months after Sonny's birth, Lucille died from kidney failure. A free wheeling railroad man, Sonny's father, couldn't possibly take care of him. And Savanna and Ava were too young to take on the responsibility. Having no children of their own, Earl and Estelle Case decided to keep Sonny and raise him as their own child. Before long Savanna was thrown out of her home and had nowhere to go. Smokey was the only person that offered her a place to live and work. Attached to his ugly, two-story frame house was a two car garage where he established his juke joint. Above the garage were two rooms which became Sassy's home. It was more than one night that she threaten to kill any man who attempted to ascend the stairway on the side of Smokey's place that led to her rooms. When Smokey passed away he left everything to Sassy. Included was his practically new two door coupe, his ugly house, $2,000 cash in his bank account and his emergency $8,000 cash that he kept in the hollow leg of his bed frame. Two parcels of land, his place of business and his most valuable possession a State Liquor License. The savvy business woman remained in the rooms above the saloon while making major renovations. She knocked out the back wall on the lower level of the house and connected the house to the garage. With the extension she added a fully functional restaurant style kitchen. A cloak room, male and female bathrooms, a bar, dining area, dance floor and a small bandstand. There was one front entrance and two back exists and an entrance was added from her house into the kitchen. The old dining room of the house served as her office. The remainder of the house also got a complete overhaul. She switched the front entrance to the left of the house, new wood siding, new windows and shutters, fresh white paint and a brick walkway made her home charming. At the front door of her house one could almost forget that a few feet on the other side was juke joint.

"So, it's just you, me, and the boys?" Sonny asked. "No, you have another Aunt, Ava," Sassy replied. "She became a live-in maid with a family over in Parsons when I left home. The family she works for moved to Virginia about twenty-five years ago, but we still keep in touch." "Where is my Father?" "I'm sorry to say that I don't know. Estelle received a card postmarked from Chicago when you were about five years old. Since then we heard nothing. I'm sure your momma knew his people or at least where they were, but we didn't. We never knew what company he worked for, and we figured he must have gotten killed doing his job. Your know working on the rails is real dangerous work?" "What happened to my grandfather?" "Oh, he died many years ago, thank the Lord." "I have blood relations?" "Yes you do, Sonny. You have your boys and you have two Aunts, me and Ava."

Chapter Twenty-Four
LENORA COMES HOME

She had been in the big city for so long and had become accustomed to fanciful things that she had forgotten the wonders of simple things. Mile after mile her old way of life came running past her through the train windows. Farms, barns, wells, pastures, fruit orchards, chicken coups, pig pens, ponds, lakes, creeks and dusty roads were a site for sore city eyes.

It was three weeks before Madeline's wedding and time for preparations was running short and every minute up until the wedding date counted. Thank goodness the train was on time. It was a toss up between Isaac and Madeline to determine which was more anxious to see Lenora. Isaac had not seen his baby girl for over five years. His marriage to Marianne and their love for each other was a true blessing, but the love for his daughter was only surpassed by his love for God. "Where is she, where is she?" he repeated to himself gazing through the windows at the passengers as the train slowed to a halt. Madeline's eagerness paralleled with Isaac's to see Lenora. They had so much to do in such little time while Lenora was on holiday. Shortly after the wedding she would be returning to New York. Madeline's head was bobbing as fast, up and down, back and fourth, as Isaacs. Ricky and Marianne stood back, looked at their partners than at each other and laughed. Partly because they looked like chickens, but so did they franticly searching the train windows for Lenora.

"Do you see her?" asked Isaac. "No," they all replied. "Where can she be?" asked Marianne. "Is this the right train?" "Yes, yes, this is it," replied Isaac, "there are no other trains tonight." Ricky spotted Lenora when she stepped off the train but decided not to let on. He wanted to watch the others reactions to her transformation. All of the passengers for the stop exited the train, and there was no one left to get off. Isaac ringing his hat in his hands walked toward the end of the train platform. All alone at the end of the platform, he saw a beautiful, well dressed, dark skinned, young lady standing with her bags. "Maybe, I should ask if she's seen my daughter?" he said to himself. "Excuse me Miss.," he said while looking at the train and partly looking at the young lady. "I am here to greet my daughter and I can't seem to find her. By any chance did you see?" Before he could finish Lenora began to giggle. "Daddy, you are speaking to your daughter," said Lenora. Isaac's heart leaped, as he turned to face the young lady. The laugh was Lenora's but the face was Lethea, no it's Lenora. "Oh, honey!" he cried, putting his arms around his baby girl. "Baby, it's you! Come look ya'll, it's Lenora." Madeline could hardly contain herself as she squealed and jumped while hugging her friend. "You look so different and you look so beautiful," she said teary eyed. "Hey you," said Ricky taking his turn at hugging his friend. Marianne said, "She looks no different to me, she's as beautiful as ever. She's now grown up and the spiting image of her mother." Marianne opened her arms to enfold her loving step daughter and said, "Welcome home."

The bridal shower was held the weekend before Lenora came home. She was originally scheduled to attend the shower but a special alumnus responsibility was assigned her. In addition, she was interviewed for an Assistant Teacher's position at Everly, which she accepted. She planned to make the announcement at her welcome home dinner on the next evening. A swatch of the white satin fabric for Madeline's wedding dress, and three different shades of blue were sent to Lenora by Madeline. It was left up to Lenora to determine which blue was best for the bridesmaids' dresses. As with most everything, they both agreed on the same color, Robin's Egg Blue. Madeline wrote: "I am so happy that you liked the fabric for my wedding dress and like Robin's Egg Blue best. The Almanac predicted great weather for the third weekend in June. It has to be great weather because the reception will be held in our backyard. I wanted to wait until your arrival to share the following, but if I withhold it any longer I'm sure I'd burst. Your father and Ricky have been corresponding about Ricky's interest in buying the store. Your father has accepted his offer on one condition. The condition is that Ricky, become his partner for a period of five years and learn the ends and outs of retailing. After the five years, Ricky will buy the store outright. Plus, and this is a big plus, your father has decided to clean the storage area over the store and fit it for living quarters for Ricky and I. This is the best part, as a wedding gift from your father and my father! Can you believe that junky space is big enough for a small kitchen, dining, living area, bathroom and bedroom? I wish you were here to help me paint and arrange the furniture. My mother, Miss. Bertha and Miss. Marianne have already begun reupholstering the sofa and two arm chairs that Miss. Victoria gave me. Yes that's right, Miss. Victoria. The dining room set is a gift from both of the Chadwell sisters. I guess Miss. Leslie had to get in on the giving too."

Even the Chadwell sisters were caught up in the excitement preparing for Lenora's homecoming. While making finger sandwiches Leslie broke out in song. She could sing at any given time her most beloved song "America the Beautiful." Her favorite verse "…and crown thy good with brotherhood from sea to shining sea." Victoria would sometime add, "uh um, brotherhood? I can't see you sharing brotherhood with old Jim Bones." "Victoria you should be ashamed of yourself," said Leslie. "Why do you have to mention him? That old man used to scare me to death. Staring at me, walking around me and jiggling the change in his pants pockets. Since we're talking about brotherhood – why don't I mention sisterhood? I can't see you sharing any sisterhood with Sister Mabel," said Leslie. "Oh, now there you go talking about that nasty hussy," Victoria replied. "I don't think she is so nasty. As a matter of fact she's quite nice, and you know that Bailey thought so too." "She's not nice and she's never been nice. If she hadn't opened her legs to my Bailey he would be here right now." "You don't know that she did that." "Yes, I do! She was always grinning up in his face. She did do it, she did! She was the one who convinced him to leave me!" "I can say no such a thing,

Victoria. And why we are still on the subject of sisterly love, sister or should I say grandmother? Why don't you show some sisterly love to Pickle Johnson and her babies?" "Now stop it, you just stop it Leslie!" "I'm just messing with you, Victoria." Leslie knew how to rattle Victoria's cage, which left her fuming. Yet not once could Victoria bring herself to broach Bailey's accusations to her sister. Not even after witnessing firsthand, on her countless sleepless nights, after her husband's abandonment, her sister's nighttime escapades. On the nights of her disappearances she was out the back door at 10:30PM and across the backyard into the thicket not retuning until 4:30AM the following morning. "Is that you sister?" Victoria called out early one morning when she heard her sister creeping up the back stairs? "Yes it is dear. I was feeling a little under the weather and decided to sit on the back porch for a little while to take in some air. I am so sorry dear ,I didn't mean to wake you. I feel so much better. Go back to sleep, Victoria, it will be time for us to get up before you know it." Victoria had watched her sister emerge from the thicket less than ten minutes beforehand. Leslie was lying to her and till this day she knew not why. What did Leslie really know about sisterly love, she thought? She was sure if Sweet Daddy was alive he would have long put a stop to Leslie's foolishness. He was the most kind and unselfish man she knew and a consummate business man. He purchased Pickers Woods and subdivided it into forty-nine plots. Before that he owned four rental properties on the Hill and an apartment house in Parsons. His foresight to sell off all of his real estate investments in 1926, except for the remaining plots in Pickers Woods and one of five rental properties on the Hill, paid off. He didn't take much to church but her father was a good man, a most respected an upstanding resident. That is why she still had an issue with Bailey stating, "He wasn't no saint!" Neither Bailey nor anyone else was going to tell her that in verity her Sweet Daddy had been a shady slumlord and a pimp. She wouldn't have believed them anyway. None of his shady dealings were ever made known to his wife or his daughters. Mrs. Chadwell went to her grave believing he was a most loving and loyal husband and father. What he couldn't collect in cash payments he collected in sexually favors from his married and unmarried female tenants alike. The apartment house in Parsons was a high end brothel effectively run by him and his woman, Isabella, until he began to feel the debilitating affects of cancer and was forced to sell it to her. Pandering with women while his wife was living and after she wasn't all came under the auspice of good business when it came to Sweet Daddy Chadwell.

Patricia hadn't had a drink in four days and it was driving her mad. She had to be clear headed and sober when she attended Lenora's coming home party this evening. "The wench had already been home for a day and had the nerve not to stop by to say, hello," she said talking to her reflection in the mirror. "She probably still can't hold a candle to me. What am I talking about? She can't and never will look as good as me? I am still the best looking woman in Kendal Grove, and she is still homely." She had at least three hours to herself before the party to prepare to look her best. Everyone else was already at the Howard's making preparation except Chaz who was out of town at a clergy meeting in Bricktown. After the meeting he would speedily drive the fifty miles straight to the party.

Hearing movement and voices in the kitchen took Patricia by surprise. She knew Madeline's voice but who did the other voice belong too? Who was referring to Bertha as Aunt Bertha? Her niece Kitty wasn't in town. "She keeps her largest serving bowl on the bottom shelf of the pantry," the unfamiliar voice said. Who is that and how would they know that? Patricia thought. Patricia put on her robe and raced to the kitchen. The swinging door squeaked as she opened it. Madeline looked passed Lenora and spoke her most distasteful word, "Patricia." "Madeline," snarled Patricia. Lenora with her back to Patricia slowly turned around to face her. "Hello, Patricia," she said. Patricia had no inkling who the gorgeous, dark skinned, full figured woman was addressing her. Than as if a mighty wave from the ocean came up and hit her in the face, it came to her. "Lenora!" Patricia couldn't believe her eyes. "Lenora it's you?" "Yes, it's me," Lenora replied. Madeline than chimed in, "We came to pick-up the serving bowl. Your mother-in-law is waiting for it. We'll see you a little later." The two friends found what seemed like a million other things to talk about except Patricia Carter on their way back to the others. Patricia was left to her own thoughts, and the thought of what she saw sent her straight to her stash of liquor. Clear headed and sober went out the window with one look at her old rival. One stiff drink was undeniably necessary. Five consecutive shots of liquor landed her back in conversation with her reflection. "Lenora looked good, no great, and she was more the beauty than I could ever be," Patricia said slamming the bottle down on her vanity table. "So what, she can't have Chaz. Oh no, what if he decides to leave me for her? He would never do that, I'm the mother of his child. Why wouldn't he? Oh no, I've got to get ready, I've got to get over there and get my husband. After one more drink."

Chaz had finally arrived from his long drive and greeted the Howard's and the other guests. He was anxiously looking forward to seeing the dearest person in his life again. His separation from Lenora and marriage to another woman never diminished his undying love for her. 'Where is she, where is she, Ricky?" he said fervently. "She hasn't come down yet," said Ricky. "Calm down Chaz, calm down." Ricky laughed out loud at his best friend, who he hadn't seen so excited since they were kids. "Daddy, Daddy," Joey said running and jumping into Chaz's arms. "Hey there big man," Chaz said to his son, "Where is your grandmother?" "She's upstairs with Aunt Marianne and Aunt Lenora." "Oh yea, maybe I should go up?" "Maybe, no you shouldn't?" said Ricky. She'll be down in a minute." Bertha and Marianne stood at the top of the staircase. "Everyone, may I have your attention," said Bertha. The guests assembled in the large foyer around the bottom of the stairs. Those that couldn't fit in the foyer strained their necks around the corner of either side. Those outside on the front porch peered through the downstairs windows. Then Marianne said, "Please join us in welcoming home our own, Lenora." Lenora stood at the top of the stairs in an off-white chiffon evening dress, with evening slippers dyed to match. Her hair was in an upsweep with curls nestled on the top of her head. She wore pearl earrings and a pearl necklace to complete her ensemble. The guests were astonished by her transformation and were zealously waiting to welcome her home. Chaz, mesmerized, gently put his son down and tried to find words but couldn't. Ricky patted Chaz's shoulder and said, "It's alright man, it's alright the words will come. Stay calm, stay calm, the words will come." Ricky assured his friend.

When Lenora reached the downstairs landing she was mobbed by her guests. Everyone wanted to hug, kiss and talk with her. With her gracious manner she greeted everybody and made each person feel as important as the next. Chaz for the first time in his life had lost his composure. He felt that if he got some air he may be able to compose himself. He walked around the house twice, and decided to take a vacant seat on the front porch where he sat and talked with the other guests for the next four hours.

The hour had become late and the majority of guests had departed. Lenora made her way to the front porch for a much needed break and to take in some air. It was finally Chaz's time. His palms were sweating, and he didn't know whether to laugh, cry or spit. All he knew was spitting was out of the question, even if he wanted too. "Lenora," he said as he took her hand into his, pulling her close intertwining their arms and kissing the back of her hand. He still had no words as he pressed the back of her hand to his cheek. He wanted to express his thoughts and what he was feeling with each breath and with each beat of his heart, I love you, I love you. But he knew it was best to keep his thoughts and feelings to himself no matter how true.

It was a clear and warm summer evening for the conclusion of an enjoyable celebration. Then they heard it. "You black bitch get away from my husband!" Patricia screeched. The guest left stirring were startled by the outburst and were turning their heads in every direction to discern who and where the outburst emanated from. Joe, James, Bertha and Chaz didn't exactly know where the outburst came from, but they recognized the voice it came from. "Get away from my husband, or I'll kill you!" Patricia shouted. Patricia arrived at the party with Bertha's best carving knife in hand. The ten inch carving knife used to slice delectable meats served at holiday meals. "Get your hands off of her, Chaz," she insisted trying to stabilize her footing on the exposed tree roots. Her pink ankle strap high heel pumps, dyed to match her pink crepe dress she wore, were no match for the track over the twisted mass of tree roots. "Keep those children in the backyard!" Someone yelled. Patricia desperately tried to balance herself against the tree. "I saw you trying to steal my husband," she said wobbling back and forth. "Patricia, you need to stop this!" Bertha said trying not to yell. Patricia, again trying to move forward, dropped the knife. "How can ya'll start a party without me being here?" she asked, vigorously pointing to herself. With the grandiose gesture, she completely lost her footing and fell onto the upright blade of the knife firmly wedged between the roots. Lenora's welcome home in turn was Patricia's final farewell.

Chapter Twenty-Five
THE CHRISTENING

The rumor of a dark skinned girl on the cover of the next issue of Circular Magazine was all the talk. Not only was she on the cover but it was to also be a full expose on the girl. There was no better way for Constance Beavin to show off her future daughter-in-law. The magazine had no choice but to meet the demands of its largest advertiser, Beavin Shoe Manufacturing Company. She couldn't have put together anyone like Lenora for Kennis if she was given all of the parts herself to assemble. No one in Harlem or anywhere else came close to that lovely young lady. The only drawback to some in their social circle, mainly the ones from the south, was her dark complexion. But if she, the Mrs. Constance Beavin, could overlook Lenora's complexion so should everyone else. The expose, she thought, would put them all in their places. Her beauty, intellect, charm and poise make men stand to their feet when she enters a room, and her benevolence bowls everyone over. It was Lenora as chair of the Everly alumnus who erected change in the organizations charitable allocations. "This year rather than the traditional effort of solely preparing fruit baskets for the elderly, I think we should do something different," Lenora said. "I propose we add an additional effort. I've taken the liberty to contact the Mission in Sparks to help those less fortunate than we are. There are young ladies there who lack basic necessities we take for granted such as undergarments, clothes, shoes and coats. There are also young mothers without food or clothing for their babies. Before we take this matter up for a vote are there any questions?" "Yes, I have one," said Gretchen. "Are you seriously asking us to go to Sparks and associate with those people?" "Yes I am," said Lenora. "Why should we help them?" asked Blanch. "We should leave them to fend for themselves. I for one wouldn't dare go there," she added. "Thank you for sharing your sentiments, Ladies. If there are no more comments or questions we can put the matter to a vote." All were in favor of working with the Sparks Mission except Gretchen, Blanch and their closest friends. Gretchen was not going to be in favor of anything Lenora brought to the table. No matter how beneficial it would be to those in need. At every opportunity she covertly railed against Lenora's motions and would undermine her with shrewd reasoning. It was the only way she could get back at her for stealing her intended, and more importantly, her place in the Circle.

The Mission workers and the Sisters of the Sparks Lodge were most appreciative for the multitude of contributions. They worked splendidly with Lenora and the other private school graduates sorting out the garments. Specially taken by Lenora was the Chair of the lodge committee Mrs. Darcine Bash and the two Co-Chairs, Dalcy Bash and her cousin Lettie Bash. After much talk and the admiration of Lenora and her gold bracelet bearing a single charm with the initials "KB" Dalcy learned they had something in common. Dalcy's boyfriend also bore the same initials.

There is no deceit or conniving in Lenora, thought Constance. She is a natural leader, which was a rare quality for most girls her age. Bringing to mind the lack of qualities exhibited by the unpleasant, Gretchen Hollis. She couldn't believe that she was set on Gretchen as her daughter-in-law. The most boring, shallow and insecure young woman she'd ever had the chance to meet. Not to mention Gretchen was varus and flat assed. All the same, with the knowledge of her deficiencies if Lenora was no longer available for any odd reason Gretchen would be the next in line to marry Kennis, due to her family name and the hefty income from their chain of funeral homes. Albeit, Lenora's family income did not compare to the Hollis' but with three Howard's Apparel stores and another opening soon, her mother's inheritance and her grandfather's inheritance, it would only be a matter of time. Gretchen was in and now she is out. Isn't that something? Constance thought.

With the wave of her hand she could admit or dismiss anyone she wanted from the upper tiers of their society. "Look at me the undisputed Queen of the Circle, is that you Fanny Barnes?" Constance said to herself. Leaning over the montage of perfume bottles on her dressing table, primping in her mirror. Like her ascent resembling that of a graduate from one of the finer finishing schools and her name, Constance Beavin was a fake. She and her sister's behavior were based on what they read in books, had seen in movies or copied, without her knowledge, from Helen Franklin who was many years their senior. Helen Franklin was a genuine lady with no pretense about her. Raised with dignity and taught at an early age the fine qualities of a lady.

Rouda and Fanny Barnes grew up in a hovel fifteen miles east of Sparks in a shanty town. Moving into one of the dilapidated apartment buildings in Sparks in those days would have been a step up for them. If it wasn't for the mysterious and handsome, dark haired, white cab driver who showed up on their doorstep one Sunday afternoon, who would have known what would have become of them. With flowers for their mother's grave and an assortment of gifts for the two little girls the man said that the gifts were from their father. When their grandmother explained that he must be mistaken because their father died days after the youngest was born his story changed. He then said that the gifts were from him who had been a close friend of their father and mother who recently died. All the same the gifts kept coming, money and the cab driver too. It was he who found them a new place to live after their grandmother's passing. He also got them a job at a flower shop. It was he who insisted they legally change their first and last names, and put any bad feelings about their past and the shanty town behind them. "You shouldn't hold it against your mother because she wasn't always there for you before she died," he said in his thick Brooklyn ascent. "It's hard for a Negro woman in this world to keep a steady job and raise two girls on her own. Thank God above you had your grandmother to help. God rest her soul. You girls got looks and personalities. All you need to do is tone it down a little, and act like ladies. Cut back on the cheek and lip rouge and don't wear cheap perfume or bows on your shoes. Some men think bows on a woman's shoes make her look cheap. Your mother was kind of ladylike, a good looking and sweet girl that Florence was, and a good cook too." Like their mother, a shade to dark to pass over the color line, when cleaned up the girls were something to behold. "You knew our mother and father well?" Rouda asked. "Yea, yea, real well," he'd say before clearing his throat and changing the subject. It was he who introduced them to two swell Negro fellows that were going places. Both former number runners, one owned two barber shops and the other was in the process of expanding his shoe shop, were smitten by the Bertell sisters Vasti and Constance. After the introduction to the men that would eventually become their husbands the cab driver was never seen or heard from again. The cab driver they resembled who had the same jaw line, nose and green eyes that they both had. She thanked God that most all the people in the Shanty town had died or moved away before they left. And those that stayed didn't have the will to amount to much and would be unable to function outside of scarcity. There was no chance of them being found out hence the standard recitation was contrived to avoid excessive questioning about their past: "It was a strenuous time for us emotionally with first the passing of our father, than our mother who died from a broken heart. Than a short time later our beloved grandmother left this world." Other than that their past was barred for discussion.

"Kennis is that you?" Constance called hearing his footsteps nearing her room. "Yes, it is mother," he said. "Where are you off to on this Friday evening?" "I'm meeting up with Milo and some others." Having the knowledge that Milo was off for the weekend with one of his married lady friends. He'd rather lie to his mother about his whereabouts than let her know he was on his way to Sparks. "You look lovely mother. Where are you and Father off to tonight?" "Your father and I have to dine with the Aldor's tonight, because we couldn't get out of it. Oh, by the way Darling, did you get a moment to talk to the magazine editor?" "Yes, I did and he said "everything was in order and the next issue will be on the stands a week from today."'" "Do you think he'll ever get over you not marrying his dreadful cousin, Gretchen, and us threatening to pull the company's advertising if he didn't run the story on Lenora?" "To be honest with you Mother, it makes no difference to me one way or the other what he feels." "You're so right, have a good evening son." Kennis was all set to propose to Lenora on her return and had no doubt that she would accept his proposal. Constance had already selected and bought the 1.50 caret weight princess cut engagement ring, as well as reserved the venue for the official proposal before Lenora left town for her friends wedding. Because of Kennis' pending engagement to Lenora he considered breaking it off with Dalcy but decided not to act rashly, and made a promise to himself to think on it again soon.

Lettie couldn't get to her cousin Dalcy's house fast enough with the newest issue of Circular Magazine. The article about that sweet girl, Lenora Howard, who worked with them at the Mission, would be featured. "Aunt Darcine, maybe, they'll have pictures of her boyfriend Kennis?" Lettie said. That way we can compare the two boys with the initials "KB." I bet her boyfriend Kennis can't hold a candle to Dalcy's boyfriend Ken." Walter clearly overheard the conversation in the next room and prayed that the day that troubled him for almost six years had not come. In the kitchen he sat smoking his pipe and squirming in his seat anxiously awaiting the outcome. He didn't know how he knew that both young men with the initials "KB" were one in the same. "That is so nice go on, go on, keep reading, Dalcy turn the page," Lettie prompted. "It goes on to say that with all of her many accomplishments and time donated to helping others the one that stands above the rest is the library she began in her former home of Kendal Grove, Maryland." "A library, what else does it say?" her mother asked setting on the edge of her seat. "It also says: "Though not official the author of the article has no reason to doubt that a marriage proposal is expected from none other than Mr. Kennis Beavin of Beavin Shoe Manufacturing Company. Miss. Howard has been seen on the arm of none other since she arrived in Harlem five years ago. This author has also learned from a very reliable source that the Beavin's have purchased a 3,000 square feet house two blocks away from the Beavin's Mansion that is undergoing renovations for the soon to be married couple. Couple pictured at the Annual Jubilee Ball, on page 20." There she was with her enchanting smile in a stunning and beautifully fitted floor length satin dress. The caption under the photograph read: "Harlem's most popular young couple, Mr. Kennis Beavin and Miss. Lenora Howard." Her broadly smiling escort, with a pencil thin mustache and clad in a fitted tuxedo, tightly embraced her at his side. It was none other than Ken, her Ken Butler! "Let us see the picture Dalcy," the women pleaded. Staring blankly at the wall across the room she calmly arose from the sofa that Kennis gave them dropping the magazine to the floor, and walked over to the newly installed telephone. "Oh no!" Her mother said passing the magazine to her niece and sitting back in her chair. Walter didn't know whether to attend to his wife or daughter. "Dalcy," he said as only a concerned and loving father could tenderly call to his distraught daughter. "Dalcy, baby are you o.k.?" She took her father's outstretched hand to assure him of her stability and with the other hand picked up the telephone receiver. "Hello operator, can you get me Miss. Reagan's boarding house on 5th Street?" she spoke into the mouth piece. It was than that her cousin Lettie said, "What are you doing, Dalcy?" "There is only one thing I can do," she replied. "Hello, Leroy, this is Dalcy would you still like to take me to the Cutters Ball?"

On the afternoon of the first Sunday in June of 1947, the Christening Ceremony for Charles Isaac Carter and Eugenia Lethea Stone took place. Best friends Chaz Carter and Ricky Stone stood side-by-side watching those who made their hearts sing. Chaz turned to his friend placed his right hand upon his shoulder and said, "Look at your little lady and my two little men. And look at the two most beautiful women in the world, who we happened to be married to. Are we not the two most blessed men in the world?" Lenora Carter and Madeline Stone stood patiently in the churchyard holding their babies while watching

Joey scramble around playing with the other children. They were awaiting indication from their husbands as to what the rest of the day would hold for them.